What A World 2

Amazing Stories from Around the Globe

Milada Broukal

Longman

What a World 2: Amazing Stories from Around the Globe

Pearson Education, 10 Bank Street, White Plains, NY 10606

Vice president, multimedia and skills: Sherry Preiss
Executive editor: Laura Le Dréan
Development editors: Andrea Bryant, Dena Daniel
Production editor: Andréa C. Basora
Vice president of domestic marketing: Kate McLoughlin
Vice president of international marketing: Bruno Paul
Production manager: Ray Keating
Senior manufacturing buyer: Nancy Flaggman
Photo research: Dana Klinek
Cover and text design: Elizabeth Carlson
Text composition: Color Associates
Text font: 12/15 New Aster

Photo credits:
Page 1, Hulton Archive/Getty Images. **Page 8,** © Corbis/Annie Griffiths Belt.
Page 15, © Corbis/John Dakers; Eye Ubiquitous. **Page 23,** © Corbis/Archivo
Iconografico, S.A. **Page 30,** © Corbis. **Page 37,** © Corbis/Kit Kittle. **Page 44,**
© Musee de Grenoble/SuperStock, Inc. **Page 52,** © Corbis. **Page 59,**
Courtesy of the Turkish Embassy, Culture and Tourism Office, Washington,
D.C.. **Page 70,** © Corbis/Charles & Josette Lenars. **Page 78,** © Corbis/Earl &
Nazima Kowall. **Page 85,** © Corbis/Owen Franken. **Page 92,** © Corbis/John-
Marshall Mantel. **Page 99,** © Corbis/Historical Picture Archive. **Page 106,**
© Corbis/Historical Picture Archive. **Page 114,** AP/Wide World Photos.
Page 122, © Corbis/Nik Wheeler. **Page 130,** © Corbis/Jeremy Horner.

Library of Congress Cataloging-in-Publication Data
Broukal, Milada.
  What a world 2 : amazing stories from around the globe / by Milada
Broukal.
      p.   cm.
  Includes index.
  ISBN 0-13-048464-4 (pbk.) — ISBN 0-13-184923-9 (pbk. + audio cd)
  1. English language—Textbooks for foreign speakers. 2. Readers.
I. Title: What a world two. II. Title.
  PE1128.B7166   2004
  428.6'4—dc22   2003027562

ISBN: 0-13-048464-4

ISBN: 0-13-184923-9 (book with audio CD)

Printed in the United States of America
    8 9 10–VHJ–08

CONTENTS

INTRODUCTION

What A World 2: Amazing Stories from Around the Globe is a high beginning reader. It is the second in a three-book series of readings for students of English as a second or foreign language. Eighteen topics have been selected for this book. Each topic is about a different person, place, or custom. The topics span history and the globe, from Louis Pasteur, to the history of Timbuktu, to the purpose of fattening rooms.

Every unit begins with a question and answers that question. Each unit contains:

- A prereading activity
- A reading passage (450–700 words)
- Topic-related vocabulary work
- Comprehension exercises, including pair work.
- Discussion questions
- A writing activity
- A spelling and punctuation activity

BEFORE YOU READ opens with a picture of the person, place, or custom featured in the unit. Prereading questions follow. Their purpose is to motivate students to read, encourage predictions about the content of the reading, and involve the students' own experiences when possible. Vocabulary can be presented as the need arises.

The **READING** passage should be first done individually by skimming for the general content. The teacher may wish to explain the bolded vocabulary words at this point. The students should then do a second, closer reading. Further reading(s) can be done aloud. If you have the Student Book with the accompanying Audio CD, you can use it in the classroom or have the students listen at home.

The two **VOCABULARY** exercises focus on the bolded words in the reading. *Meaning*, a definition exercise, encourages students to work out the meanings from the context. Within this group are *Words That Go Together*—collocations or groups of words which are easier to learn together the way they are used in the language. The second exercise, *Use*, reinforces the vocabulary further by making students use the words in a meaningful, yet possibly different, context. This section can be done during or after the reading phase, or both.

There are several **COMPREHENSION** exercises. Each unit contains *Understanding the Reading*, *Remembering Details*, and *Making Inferences*. All confirm the content of the text either in general or in detail. These exercises for developing reading skills can be done individually, in pairs, in small groups, or as a class. It is preferable to do these exercises in conjunction with the text, since they are not meant to test memory. The comprehension exercises end with *Tell the Story*, which is a speaking activity.

DISCUSSION questions encourage students to bring their own ideas and imagination to the related topics in each reading. They can also provide insights into cultural similarities and differences.

WRITING provides the stimulus for students to write sentences or a short paragraph about the reading. Teachers should use their own discretion when deciding whether or not to correct the writing exercises.

SPELLING AND PUNCTUATION provides basic rules and accompanying activities for spelling or punctuation, using examples from the readings. An index listing the spelling and punctuation activities can be found on page 148.

SELF-TESTS after Unit 9 and Unit 18 review sentence structure, vocabulary, and spelling and punctuation in a multiple-choice format.

If you would like the Answer Key for *What A World 2*, please contact Pearson Longman. Customers in the United States: ESLSampling@pearsoned.com
Customers outside the United States: elt@pearsoned.com

UNIT 1

Who Is the Most Important Person from History?

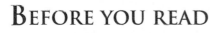

BEFORE YOU READ

Answer these questions.

1. What do you think is the most important invention in history?
2. What do you think the machine in the picture does?
3. Were books always easy to make and to get? Why or why not?

Who Is the Most
Important Person from History?

1 What person from history has the greatest **effect** on our lives today? Recently, a group of many different experts decided it was a man named Johann Gutenberg. Gutenberg is famous for inventing printing, but he didn't really invent it. He invented a better way of printing.

2 For hundreds of years people used blocks of wood to print. They used a knife to cut words in the block of wood. They made the words **backward**. Then they covered the block with ink and **pressed** it onto paper. When they pulled the paper from the inky blocks, the words appeared on the paper in the right direction. In Korea and China, people printed with metal stamps instead of wood. Either way, printing was difficult and very slow. People usually wrote books **by hand**, so it took several years to make one copy of a book.

3 Books were very expensive and **rare**. Only rich people could buy them, and only rich people could read. As more people learned to read, books became more popular. People around the world wanted to find a quicker, better, and less expensive way to print books. One of these people was Johann Gutenberg.

4 Gutenberg was born in Mainz, Germany, around 1400. We do not know the exact year. He was an intelligent man, and he was good at working with metal. Gutenberg probably **had no idea** how people printed in China. His idea was to make a metal stamp for each letter of the alphabet and use the letters **over and over**. He could put the stamps together to make words and **arrange** the words to make pages. With ink on the stamps, he could press paper on them to make a page. A "printing press" machine could make hundreds of copies of a single page quickly. After that page, he could rearrange the same letters to make other words and print other pages.

5 It took Gutenberg many years to make the stamps for each letter of the alphabet. When he finished the stamps, he didn't have enough money to make the printing press. He **borrowed** money from a man named Johann Fust. They became business **partners**. After many years, Gutenberg's printing press was ready. Gutenberg printed his first book, the Bible, around 1455.

6 Johann Fust was a good businessman. He understood the importance of Gutenberg's invention. He **took** Gutenberg **to court** because Gutenberg still owed him money. Gutenberg had no money, so Fust took his printing press and started his own business. He printed and sold more Bibles and kept all the money. Gutenberg was sad and **broke**. He died in 1468, a poor man.

7 Today people remember Johann Gutenberg. The city of Mainz has a **statue** of him and a museum. His original printing press is in the museum. They print several pages a day to show that it is still in good condition. There are only forty-eight copies of the original Bible. It is the most expensive book in the world. In 1987, a Gutenberg Bible sold in New York for $5.3 million.

VOCABULARY

MEANING

Write the correct words in the blanks.

| backward | rare | broke | pressed | effect |
| partners | statue | borrowed | arranged | |

1. Gutenberg _____ money from Johann Fust and said he would give it back later.

2. There were few books before the printing press. Books were

   _____.

3. Gutenberg _____ words to make pages, then printed the pages.

4. Gutenberg's invention was very important. It has a big _____ on our lives today.

5. People cut words _____ into blocks of wood so that the printed words would be in the right direction.

6. Gutenberg and Fust worked together and became _____ in business.

7. Before Gutenberg's printing press, people _____ blocks of wood on paper to print a page.

8. Later in his life, Gutenberg had no money and was _____.

9. The people of Mainz, Germany, wanted to remember Gutenberg, so they put a _____ of him there.

WORDS THAT GO TOGETHER

Write the correct words in the blanks.

by hand	had no idea	over and over	took . . . to court

1. The Chinese also printed on paper, but Gutenberg _____ of this. He didn't know about it.

2. They used the metal stamps not just one time, but _____.

3. Before the printing press, people copied books _____.

4. Fust wanted his money back from Gutenberg. He needed help from a judge and a lawyer. He _____ Gutenberg _____.

USE

Work with a partner to answer the questions. Use complete sentences.

1. What do you sometimes *borrow* from another student? From a neighbor?

2. What is the name of a famous *statue*? Where is it? Why is it famous?

3. What is something that is *rare*?

4. What things do you usually *press* with your finger?

5. What is something you do *over and over* in your English class? At home?

6. What things were made by hand many years ago and today are made by machines?

COMPREHENSION

UNDERSTANDING THE READING

Circle the letter of the correct answer.

1. Before Gutenberg's printing press, _____.

    a. there were other kinds of printing

    b. it was easy to print books by hand

    c. Europeans printed with metal stamps

    d. people only wrote books by hand

2. Gutenberg _____.

    a. had the idea for a printing press

    b. knew about printing in China

    c. had the idea for printing

    d. was good at working with paper

3. Today people think of Gutenberg as _____.

    a. a statue in Mainz, Germany

    b. a great inventor

    c. a great seller of Bibles

    d. sad and broke

REMEMBERING DETAILS

Reread the passage and answer the questions.

1. Where was Gutenberg born?
2. What was he good at?
3. Who did he borrow money from?
4. When did Gutenberg print his first book?
5. Where is Gutenberg's printing press?
6. How much did a Gutenberg Bible sell for recently?

MAKING INFERENCES

All of the statements below are true. Some of them are stated directly in the reading. Others can be inferred, or guessed, from the reading. Write *S* for each stated fact. Write *I* for each inference.

Example: __S__ Gutenberg invented a better way of printing.

        __I__ Before Gutenberg's time, most average people could not read.

____ 1. Gutenberg was not a good businessman.

____ 2. Gutenberg spent most of his life and money making his printing press.

____ 3. Gutenberg had no idea that his invention would have an effect on our lives today.

____ 4. The Bible was the most important book in Europe at that time.

____ 5. The Bible was the first book to be printed.

TELL THE STORY

Work with a partner or together as a class. Tell the story of Johann Gutenberg. Use your own words. Your partner or other students can ask questions about the story.

DISCUSSION

Discuss the answers to these questions with your classmates.

1. Who are some other people from history who have an effect on our lives today?
2. What is an invention that you could not live without?
3. What do you think will be the next great invention?

WRITING

Write six sentences or a short paragraph about an invention that is important to your life.

Example: *The most important invention for me is the telephone. I use the telephone many times a day to talk to my family.*

_____

_____

_____

_____

_____

_____

SPELLING AND PUNCTUATION

SILENT LETTERS: *K* AND *W*

The Silent *k*

The silent *k* usually comes at the beginning of a word and is followed by the letter *n*

*They used a **kn**ife to cut words in the block of wood.*

The Silent *w*

The silent *w* usually comes at the beginning of a word and is followed by the letter *r*.

*People usually **wr**ote books by hand.*

A. Circle the correctly spelled word in each group. You may use a dictionary.

1. rist   wrist   rwist   4. nit   knit   nkit
2. nee   nkee   knee   5. rinkle   rwinkle   wrinkle
3. knock   nock   nkock   6. wrob   rob   rwob

B. Complete the words with *kn, n, wr,* or *r*.

1. In Gutenberg's time, people ___ote books by hand.
2. Gutenberg had no ___owledge of printing in China.
3. Fust ___ew he could make money from the ___ew invention.
4. People ___eeded books to ___ead.
5. Only the ___ich could ___ead and ___ite.
6. ___iters were happy about the printing press because their books could ___each more people.
7. We ___ow ___ow the importance of Gutenberg's invention.

C. Write sentences using the words you circled in Part A.

_____

_____

_____

_____

_____

_____

UNIT 2

What Are Fattening Rooms?

BEFORE YOU READ

Answer these questions.

1. Do women in Europe and North America prefer to be thin or fat?
2. Do you think a thin person is healthier than a fat person?
3. Is it easier for you to gain weight (become fatter) or to lose weight (become slimmer)?

What Are Fattening Rooms?

1 In North America and Europe, most women want to be **slim**. In those places, a slim woman is a beautiful woman. People think that a slim woman is healthy and careful about what she eats. But in some parts of the world, women want to be fat. In many parts of Africa, a fat woman is a beautiful woman. How fat? There is no **limit**. If a woman is fat, they think that she is healthy and rich. If you are slim, that means you are a worker with little money and not enough food to eat. Also, people believe that a slim woman will be sick or that she can't have children. A fat woman has enough food to eat, so she is healthy and will have many healthy babies.

2 To help girls and women look healthy and beautiful, people in central Africa send them to a fattening room. Fattening rooms are an old tradition and an important part of a girl's life. After a girl goes to a fattening room, her family and her village say that she is a woman. The fattening room is usually near the family's house or part of it. In the fattening room, a girl sits on a special chair until it is time to eat. Then she sits on the floor on a **mat** made of leaves. She also sleeps on the floor. Her mother gives her bowls of food like rice, yams, and beans—the **kinds of** foods that help her get fat. She also drinks a lot of water.

3 In the fattening room, the girl does not move very much. She can only eat, sleep, and get fatter. Her only visitors are women who teach her how to sit, walk, and talk in front of her **future** husband. They also give her advice about cleaning, sewing, and cooking. It is boring to be in the fattening room for so long with nothing to do, but the girl **doesn't mind**. She knows that it is important for her.

4 In southeastern Nigeria, brides go to a fattening room or a fattening farm before they get married. They cannot leave the farm for many weeks. At the end of this time, but before the wedding, the brides walk through the village so everyone can **admire** their big bodies. After a woman is married, she can also go to a fattening room. She may go several times because it is important for her to stay fat. A man wants his wife to be fat so other people will think that the man is rich and that he is a **responsible** man.

(continued)

5 If parents don't send their daughter to a fattening room, their friends and relatives may laugh at them. They will say that the parents are not **doing their duty**. **In the old days**, girls sometimes stayed in a fattening room for two years. Today some families cannot **afford** more than a few months. Also, fattening rooms are not very popular in cities now. In cities, health education and Western culture have a big effect on people's ideas. But in villages, this traditional custom continues.

6 In Niger, they have a festival to celebrate the heaviest woman. Here, women have a **contest** to see who is the fattest. On the morning of the contest, the women eat **enormous** amounts of food and drink lots of water. The fattest woman is the winner. She gets a prize—more food!

VOCABULARY

MEANING

Write the correct words in the blanks.

enormous	slim	afford	contest	admire
responsible	mat	future	limit	

1. In North America and Europe, women don't want to be fat; they want to be _____.

2. In some parts of Africa, women like to be fat. There is no _____ to how fat a woman can be.

3. In a fattening room, a girl sits on a _____ on the floor when she eats.

4. Women teach her how to act in front of the man she is going to marry. She learns how to act for her _____ husband.

5. People in the village like the big bodies of the women very much. They _____ the women.

6. When a woman is fat, people think that her husband is a _____ man because he takes care of her.

7. Some families cannot _____ to keep a girl in a fattening room for a long time because it is expensive.

8. In Niger, many women want to be the fattest woman, so they have a

   _____.

9. Women eat _____ amounts of food to get fat.

WORDS THAT GO TOGETHER

Write the correct words in the blanks.

kinds of	doesn't mind	doing their duty	in the old days

1. The girl is bored in the fattening room, but she _____. She knows the fattening room is important for her life.

2. In the fattening room, girls eat the _____ foods that help make them fat.

3. _____, girls stayed in a fattening room for a long time, but today they only stay for a few months.

4. If parents don't send their daughters to fattening rooms, people will say they are not helping their daughters. People think the parents are not

   _____.

USE

Work with a partner to answer the questions. Use complete sentences.

1. Where would you like to go on a *future* vacation?
2. What quality do you *admire* in a man or woman?
3. What can't you *afford* to buy this year?
4. What are some kinds of *contests* in your country?
5. What must you do to be *slim*?
6. What *kinds of* exercise do you enjoy most?

What Are Fattening Rooms?   11

COMPREHENSION

UNDERSTANDING THE READING

Circle the letter of the correct answer.

1. In some parts of Africa, people think a slim girl _____.
   a. is healthy
   b. will have many babies
   c. is not healthy
   d. is beautiful

2. A girl goes to a fattening room _____.
   a. only to learn to sew and cook
   b. to become a woman
   c. for one week only
   d. to be alone and think

3. Today fattening rooms _____.
   a. are still popular in villages
   b. are not popular anymore
   c. are popular in villages and big cities
   d. are only popular with very rich families

REMEMBERING DETAILS

Reread the passage and fill in the blanks.

1. In some parts of Africa, people believe that a slim girl will be
   _____.

2. In the fattening room, the girl sleeps on the _____.

3. Women visitors give her advice about _____,
   _____, and _____.

4. When a man has a fat wife, people think he is a rich and
   _____ man.

5. Today fattening rooms are not popular in _____.

6. In a contest in Niger, the heaviest woman is the _____.

All of the statements below are true. Some of them are stated directly in the reading. Others can be inferred, or guessed, from the reading. Write *S* for each stated fact. Write *I* for each inference.

_____ 1. In villages, girls still go to fattening rooms.

_____ 2. A woman with an education will probably not go to a fattening room.

_____ 3. A woman may go to a fattening room several times in her life.

_____ 4. In some countries, a fat body means that the person is rich.

_____ 5. Rich men usually marry women from rich families.

TELL THE STORY

Work with a partner or together as a class. Tell the story of fattening rooms. Use your own words. Your partner or other students can ask questions about the story.

DISCUSSION

Discuss the answers to these questions with your classmates.

1. What kinds of things do people do to change their bodies? Which of these can be bad for their health?

2. What makes a man or a woman attractive in your country?

3. A person's size is not important, but in some societies people still think it is important. How can we change our society to accept people of different sizes?

WRITING

Write six sentences or a short paragraph about how you try to stay healthy and look good.

Example: *I don't eat many cakes and cookies because I don't want to gain weight.*
I try to eat fruits and vegetables.
I don't go to a gym, but I walk a lot.

_____

_____

_____

_____

_____

SPELLING AND PUNCTUATION

SUFFIXES: DOUBLING CONSONANTS IN ONE-SYLLABLE WORDS

A *suffix* is a letter or group of letters that we add to the end of a word to change its meaning or its form. We usually double the consonant in a one-syllable word with a short vowel sound before adding a suffix beginning with a vowel. Some of these suffixes are *–y, –ing, –er, –est,* and *–ed.*

fat + –er = **fatter**	*fat + –est =* **fattest**
slim + –er = **slimmer**	*slim + –est =* **slimmest**
win + –er = **winner**	*win + –ing =* **winning**

A. Underline the misspelled words. Write the correct words on the lines. Some sentences have more than one incorrect word.

1. You can see some of the bigest women in Niger. _____

2. On her wedding day, it was hot and suny. _____

3. Her parents are planing to put her in a fatening room this year.

   _____

4. She is geting ready to be a bride. _____

5. She is siting on a special chair in the fatening room.

   _____

6. Eatting a lot of food will make her the winer. _____

7. In the United States, women spend a lot of time on sliming exercises.

   _____

8. What are we eatting for dinner? _____

9. She stoped walking and runing to put on weight.

   _____

10. She was hopping to win the contest. _____

B. Write two sentences with words you corrected in Part A.

_____

_____

14   UNIT 2

UNIT 3

Where Do People Celebrate Girls' Day and Boys' Day?

BEFORE YOU READ

Answer these questions.

1. What holiday do children like most in your country?
2. What kinds of things do parents do for children on holidays?
3. What holiday do adults like most? Why?

Where Do People Celebrate Girls' Day and Boys' Day?

1 People in every country love their children. They celebrate them on their birthdays or name days. In Japan, there are **national** festivals to celebrate their children at the same time. These festivals are called Girls' Day and Boys' Day.

2 Girls' Day is also called the **Doll** Festival. The Japanese celebrate it on March 3 (the **third** day of the third month). On this day, a girl's parents prepare a table in the best room in the house. They put a red cloth on the table. Then they put steps on the table. They arrange a **set of** fifteen special dolls on the steps. Each doll has its place on the steps. The dolls **represent** the royal family in ancient Japan—emperors, empresses, ministers, and famous musicians. The emperor and empress are on the top step.

3 These are not dolls for children to play with. They are expensive. An inexpensive set of dolls can cost $200. The most popular sets cost about $700. The prices can go up to thousands of dollars. Many grandparents buy a set of dolls for their first granddaughter. When they have more granddaughters, they buy other things to put with the table, such as small pieces of furniture. Some families buy one or two pieces of furniture or dolls each year to add to their **collection**.

4 In the festival, many girls wear the traditional kimono. They have parties with their friends and eat rice cakes and drink a special rice wine. The wine has no alcohol in it, so children can drink it. After the party, the family has a traditional dinner for the girls in the family.

5 Two months after Girls' Day, on May 5, the Japanese celebrate Boys' Day. Today they call it Children's Day. People fly banners on their houses. The banners are made of paper or cloth, and they **look like** fish. When the wind blows, the fish fill with air and seem to be swimming. Each family puts up one fish for each boy. The fish of the oldest boy is the largest, and it is on top. The youngest boy has the smallest fish at the bottom. These banners represent a type of fish called the carp. The carp is a strong and **brave** fish. It swims up the river against great difficulties and doesn't **give up**. People hope the boys will grow to be strong and brave like the carp.

6 Inside the house, in a place everyone can see, there are Boys' Day dolls. These dolls represent famous soldiers and heroes in history. The boys sometimes wear **costumes** of soldiers, too. Rich families may put out old family **souvenirs**. They may also put out **swords**. The iris is an important flower on Boys' Day because its leaves look like a sword. They put iris leaves around the table with the dolls. They also add iris leaves to a hot bath. They believe that when you **take a bath** with iris leaves, it will protect you from sickness.

7 Japanese children are very happy on Girls' Day and Boys' Day, and they love these celebrations for many reasons. But the biggest reason is because there is no school!

VOCABULARY

MEANING

What is the best meaning of the underlined words? Circle the letter of the correct answer.

1. The Japanese have <u>national</u> festivals to celebrate their children.
   a. all over the country
   b. all over the city
   c. all over the world
   d. famous for a person

2. Girls' Day is also called the <u>doll</u> festival.
   a. small toy that looks like a person or baby
   b. small toy that looks like an animal
   c. small house that looks like a palace
   d. small piece of furniture

3. March is the <u>third</u> month of the year.
   a. last
   b. next after second
   c. next after first
   d. before second

4. The dolls <u>represent</u> the royal family in ancient Japan.

    a. go with

    b. are symbols of

    c. take care of

    d. are responsible for

5. The family buys dolls for their <u>collection</u>.

    a. a group of people who like to do the same hobby

    b. a group of people who are in the same family

    c. a group of objects that someone puts together as a hobby

    d. a group of toys for boys or girls of the same age

6. The carp is a <u>brave</u> fish.

    a. not afraid

    b. big

    c. tasty

    d. not old

7. The boys sometimes wear <u>costumes</u> of soldiers.

    a. clothes of a different time or place

    b. heavy clothes to keep warm

    c. old clothes that nobody wants

    d. new clothes that go together

8. Rich families show their old family <u>souvenirs</u>.

    a. old pieces of furniture

    b. objects that make you remember a place or a time

    c. objects that are worth a lot of money

    d. objects that you don't want others to see

9. The leaf of the iris flower looks like a <u>sword</u>.

    a. a big fish that is brave

    b. a long knife

    c. a kind of doll

    d. a kind of stone

What is the best meaning of the underlined words? Circle the letter of the correct answer.

1. They believe that if you <u>take a bath</u> with iris leaves, you will not get sick.
   a. wash your face only
   b. wash your hair only
   c. wash your clothes
   d. wash your body

2. The carp swims against great difficulties and doesn't <u>give up</u>.
   a. take a rest
   b. die quickly
   c. stop trying
   d. slow down

3. The banners <u>look like</u> fish.
   a. move in the same way as
   b. are not the same as
   c. appear similar to
   d. swim in the same way as

4. They arrange a <u>set of</u> fifteen dolls on steps.
   a. a group of things that are different
   b. a group of things that go together
   c. a group of things that are new
   d. a group of things for children

USE

Work with a partner to answer the questions. Use complete sentences.

1. What is the name of a *national* festival in your country?
2. What is the name of the *third* month of the year in English?
3. What kind of *souvenirs* do you buy when you are on vacation?
4. When do people wear *costumes*?
5. What do you have a *set of* at home? (for example, kitchen knives)
6. When is it important not to *give up*? When is it okay to give up?

COMPREHENSION

UNDERSTANDING THE READING

Circle the letter of the correct answer.

1. In Japan, _____.
   a. only rich children have festivals
   b. there are special days for boys and girls
   c. boys and girls don't celebrate birthdays
   d. boys and girls don't like festivals

2. On Girls' Day, girls' parents _____.
   a. prepare a special table with dolls
   b. dress their girls like dolls
   c. buy a new set of dolls every year
   d. let girls play with dolls

3. On Boys' Day, boys' parents _____.
   a. wear costumes
   b. give their sons fish to eat
   c. fly banners of swords
   d. fly banners of fish for their sons

REMEMBERING DETAILS

Reread the passage and fill in the blanks.

1. On Girls' Day, parents cover the table with a red _____.
2. They put a set of _____ on the steps.
3. Today they call Boys' Day _____.
4. The banners on top of houses look like _____.
5. The leaves of the iris flower look like _____.
6. On Girls' Day and Boys' Day, there is no _____.

MAKING INFERENCES

All of the statements below are true. Some of them are stated directly in the reading. Others can be inferred, or guessed, from the reading. Write *S* for each stated fact. Write *I* for each inference.

_____ 1. The Japanese have a long history.

_____ 2. There are dolls of soldiers on Boys' Day.

_____ 3. The biggest fish banner is for the oldest boy.

_____ 4. The Japanese like to use symbols.

_____ 5. The dolls for Girls' Day and Boys' Day are expensive.

TELL THE STORY

Work with a partner or together as a class. Tell the story of Girls' Day and Boys' Day. Use your own words. Your partner or other students can ask questions about the story.

DISCUSSION

Discuss the answers to these questions with your classmates.

1. Do you think every country should have a Girls' Day and a Boys' Day? Why or why not?

2. How do you think people would celebrate Girls' Day and Boys' Day in your country?

3. What special day or festival would you like to have? How should people celebrate it?

WRITING

Write six sentences or a short paragraph about what you or your family do to celebrate a special day for someone else.

Example: *I always buy a birthday card for my sister. I also buy her a gift and wrap the gift in special paper.*

_____

_____

_____

_____

_____

_____

SPELLING AND PUNCTUATION

WORDS WITH THE SAME SOUNDS

Some words have the same sounds, but they have different meanings and spellings. These words are called *homonyms*.

two	**Two** months after Girls' Day, the Japanese celebrate Boys' Day.
too	The boys sometimes wear costumes of soldiers, **too.**
to	They add iris leaves **to** a hot bath.
their	They have parties with **their** friends.
they're	**They're** happy on this day.
there	**There** is no school.
its	**Its** leaves look like a sword.
it's	**It's** an old celebration.

Circle the correct word for each sentence.

1. People like to celebrate (they're/their) birthdays.
2. The Japanese have (two/too) special days for children.
3. (There/They're) Girls' Day and Boys' Day.
4. (Its/It's) March 3 today.
5. The doll has (its/it's) place on the steps.
6. On Children's Day, people fly banners on (their/they're) houses.
7. The banners are of the carp. (It's/Its) a brave fish.
8. The iris is a special flower. They put (its/it's) leaves in a bath.
9. The girls have a special day and the boys have a special day, (two/too).
10. Grandparents give their granddaughters one or (two/too) pieces of furniture.

UNIT 4

Why Is Marco Polo Famous?

BEFORE YOU READ

Answer these questions.

1. Who are some famous explorers or travelers?
2. What kinds of things can you learn when you travel to other countries?
3. What are some foods you know that came from other countries? For example, pizza comes from Italy, but people all over the world eat it.

Why Is Marco Polo Famous?

1 Marco Polo was not the first European to travel to China, but he was the first to write about his travels. At that time, China was an unknown and **romantic** land to Europeans. Some people didn't believe it was a real place. Marco Polo helped them see the world as a much bigger and more interesting place.

2 Marco Polo was born in Venice in 1254. His father, Niccolo Polo, was a businessman and traveled away from home often. In 1265, Marco's father and uncle, Maffeo, decided to go to China. They were the first Europeans to travel there. In China, they met the emperor, Kublai Khan. The emperor thought the Europeans were interesting and **invited** them to return. The brothers went back to Italy and told Marco about their **adventures**. The brothers wanted to return to China, and this time they took seventeen-year-old Marco with them.

3 The three men left again for China in 1271. China was thousands of miles away from Venice. First they went by ship to the Mediterranean **coast** of Turkey. Then they went on land and **passed through** what is today Iran and Afghanistan. They crossed deserts and mountains and rivers. They had to travel for three years.

4 When they finally **reached** China, the emperor Kublai Khan welcomed his old friends and the young man with them. Marco was a good student of languages, and soon he learned Chinese. Kublai Khan liked Marco Polo and gave him a job. He traveled all over the country to represent the emperor. Marco saw beautiful things and met many people. He wrote about all of this later. The Polos had a good life in China, but after seventeen years there, they wanted to return to Italy.

5 In Italy, Marco couldn't **settle down**. He became the captain of a ship because he wanted to continue his travels. Soon Venice **went to war** with Genoa, another Italian city. Marco and his ship joined the war. Venice lost, and Marco Polo became a **prisoner** in Genoa.

6 Marco shared his room in the prison with a man named Rustichello da Pisa. They **passed the time** by talking about their lives. Polo talked about his travels and his life in China. Rustichello loved Polo's stories. He was a writer, so he helped Marco write down his stories in a book. The **title** of the book in English is *The Travels of Marco Polo*.

7 In the book, Polo **describes** the cities he saw, the people he met, and the way people lived. He describes animals, plants, and things that people used. He describes paper money, gunpowder, and porcelain vases. People in Europe didn't know about these things. They didn't want to believe that the world was so different in other places. They said Marco Polo's stories were not true. They called him "Il Milione," the man of a million lies. Before he died in 1324, Marco Polo said, "I didn't write about half of the things that I saw." He knew no one believed him.

8 It took a long time, but people finally learned that Marco Polo's stories were mostly true. Many explorers used Polo's book as a **guide**. Christopher Columbus read it before he made his first trip to the New World.

VOCABULARY

MEANING

Write the correct words in the blanks.

reached	coast	describes	guide	title
prisoner	romantic	invited	adventures	

1. The emperor of China _____ Marco's father and uncle to come back to his country.
2. Marco's father and uncle took a long, exciting trip. When they returned, they told people about their _____.
3. The Polos saw Turkey from their ship. They saw the _____ of Turkey.
4. The Polos traveled for three years. They finally _____ China.
5. Some people in Genoa took Marco Polo away and kept him in jail. He was a _____.
6. Marco Polo's book tells what China was like. It _____ China.
7. The _____ of the book is *The Travels of Marco Polo*.
8. People did not know much about faraway places at that time, so travelers used Marco Polo's book as a _____.
9. People thought China was not real. It was only a _____ place they could dream about.

WORDS THAT GO TOGETHER

Write the correct words in the blanks.

went to war	passed the time	settle down	passed through

1. The Polos _____ many countries on their way to China.
2. Marco liked to travel all the time. He didn't want to

   _____.
3. The city of Venice and the city of Genoa had problems and fights. They

   _____ with each other.
4. Marco and Rustichello did different things in prison. They

   _____ by talking about their lives and writing stories.

USE

Work with a partner to answer the questions. Use complete sentences.

1. What is the *title* of a book you like?
2. What food or drink do you give people who you *invite* to your home?
3. How would you *describe* your classroom?
4. How do you *pass the time* on weekends?
5. Where do you want to *settle down*?
6. Why do countries *go to war*?
7. What is the name of a town on the coast of your country or another country?

COMPREHENSION

UNDERSTANDING THE READING

Circle the letter of the correct answer.

1. Marco Polo _____.
   a. was the first person to travel to China
   b. and his father and uncle were the first people to travel to China
   c. was the first person to write about his travels to China
   d. was the first romantic person to travel to China

2. Marco Polo _____.

    a. was a prisoner in China

    b. had a good life in China

    c. had a good life when he returned from China

    d. was a captain of a ship in China

3. People _____.

    a. hated Marco's stories

    b. thought Marco's stories were boring

    c. did not believe Marco's stories

    d. thought Rustichello went to China

REMEMBERING DETAILS

Reread the passage and answer the questions.

1. How old was Marco Polo when he went to China?
2. How long did it take to get to China?
3. What did Marco Polo do for the emperor in China?
4. How long did the Polos stay in China?
5. Why did Marco Polo become the captain of a ship?
6. What famous explorer used Marco Polo's book as a guide?

MAKING INFERENCES

All of the statements below are true. Some of them are stated directly in the reading. Others can be inferred, or guessed, from the reading. Write _S_ for each stated fact. Write _I_ for each inference.

_____ 1. In Marco Polo's time, people thought China was a faraway, romantic place.

_____ 2. In China, Marco Polo knew what to say and do in difficult situations.

_____ 3. The Polos liked China, but they wanted to return to their home.

_____ 4. Without Rustichello, there would not be a book about Polo's travels.

_____ 5. Marco Polo knew people did not believe his stories.

TELL THE STORY

Work with a partner together or as a class. Tell the story of Marco Polo. Use your own words. Your partner or other students can ask questions about the story.

DISCUSSION

Discuss the answers to these questions with your classmates.

1. What interesting things do you know about life in other countries?
2. Some people like to travel to other countries, but others don't. Which kind of person are you? Why?
3. In the past, travel was slow and difficult. Describe travel today. Do we have travel problems today that Marco Polo did not have?

WRITING

Write six sentences or a short paragraph about a place you traveled to and what you saw.

Example: *Last year, I went to London. I saw red buses and black taxi cabs.*

_____

_____

_____

_____

_____

_____

SPELLING AND PUNCTUATION

CAPITAL LETTERS: TITLES OF RELATIONSHIP

Use a capital letter for words like *uncle* or *grandma* when they are used as a name or part of a person's name.

*Marco wanted to go with his **Uncle** Maffeo.*

When a possessive pronoun (*my, his, her, their*) comes before a word like *uncle* or *grandma*, we do <u>not</u> use a capital letter.

*Every time my **uncle** visits, he brings me a gift.*

A. Write *C* for sentences with the correct capital letters. Rewrite the incorrect sentences.

1. Marco traveled with his father and uncle.

   _____

2. Marco's mother died when he was sixteen.

   _____

3. The brothers loved to travel.

   _____

4. His father and uncle matteo traveled to China before.

   _____

5. They went to visit cousin Mario in Florence.

   _____

6. My two cousins live in Italy.

   _____

7. When Marco returned from China his aunt did not recognize him.

   _____

8. My dad and I are traveling to China this year.

   _____

9. We always stay at grandma Teresa's house when we go on vacation in Italy.

   _____

10. She and grandpa have lived there for forty years.

    _____

B. Write two sentences with titles of relationship.

   _____

   _____

UNIT 5

Who Reached the South Pole First?

Capt. R. Amundsen
Arctic Explorer

Copyright 1906
By C. L. Andrews

BEFORE YOU READ

Answer these questions.

1. What is the coldest place you ever visited?
2. What qualities must you have to be an explorer?
3. What place or thing would you like to explore? (for example, the Andes, a cave)

Who Reached the South Pole First?

1 In 1900, there were two places in the world that were not explored. These were lands of snow and ice—the North Pole and the South Pole.

2 As a young man in Norway, Roald Amundsen read about explorers who tried to reach the North Pole, and he wanted to reach it, too. It became his dream. The first step was to learn how to sail, so Amundsen went to sea as a worker on a ship when he was twenty-two. Later, he worked on a ship that went to Antarctica. Antarctica is the coldest place on Earth. The South Pole is in the center of Antarctica. It was an exciting trip, but they did not reach the South Pole.

3 He sailed on many ships and **worked his way up** to the top jobs. In 1903, he was the captain of a ship **on its way** to the Arctic. This ship was the first to sail the Northwest Passage. The Northwest Passage was important because it helped people to travel from Europe to Asia.

4 Amundsen was now a famous explorer, and he started to plan his **voyage** to the North Pole. Then he learned that an American named Robert Peary was **already** there. Amundsen wanted to be first, so he changed his plans and went to the South Pole **instead**. He heard that an English explorer named Robert Scott was on his way to the South Pole, so Amundsen sent him a message. He said that this was now a **race**.

5 When Amundsen reached Antarctica, he and four of his men started toward the South Pole. There was only ice and snow, and the wind was freezing. He had teams of dogs to pull sleds with food and tents. They climbed mountains of snow and fell through holes in the ice. Finally, they were near the South Pole. They didn't know **whether** Scott was already there. They reached the South Pole on December 14, 1911, and there was **no sign of** Scott. Amundsen won the race.

6 Scott and his group were on their way, but they were not prepared for the **extreme** weather. They did not have the right clothes, and Scott had horses instead of dogs. The horses were not **used to** the freezing weather of Antarctica, and the men had to shoot them. The men then had to carry everything. Scott and his men finally arrived at the South Pole, but thirty-three days after Amundsen's group. Scott saw the Norwegian flag and was sad. He and his men returned to their camp. On the way, one man died. At the camp the four men didn't have **fuel** for heat.

(*continued*)

7 People around the world were very happy for Amundsen, but they wanted to know whether Scott and his men also reached the South Pole. They waited many months, but there was no news. The next summer, another group of people went to look for them. They finally found the camp and the bodies of Scott and his men in their tent. They were all frozen.

8 Amundsen reached the South Pole, but he still had the **goal** to go to the North Pole. In 1926, he and his friend Umberto Nobile flew in an airship over the North Pole—another first! A few years later, Nobile's airship crashed on another Arctic trip. Amundsen went to search for him. On the way, his airplane crashed, and the great explorer died. Other people found Nobile later—he **survived**.

VOCABULARY

MEANING

Write the correct words in the blanks.

extreme	survived	whether	goal	fuel
voyage	already	instead	race	

1. Amundsen wanted to travel to the North Pole. He went on a _____.

2. Amundsen heard that another person was at the North Pole first. The person was _____ there.

3. Amundsen and Scott had a _____ to see who would reach the South Pole first.

4. Amundsen didn't know _____ Scott was already at the South Pole.

5. The weather in the South Pole was very, very cold. It was too _____ for horses.

6. Scott and his men froze to death because they had no _____ for heat.

7. After the South Pole, Amundsen decided to reach his original _____, the North Pole.

8. Amundsen died, but his friend Nobile didn't die. He _____.

9. Amundsen wanted to go to the North Pole, but he changed his plans and went to the South Pole _____.

WORDS THAT GO TOGETHER

Write the correct words in the blanks.

on its way	no sign of	used to	worked his way up

1. Amundsen got to the South Pole and didn't see Scott. There was _____ Scott.
2. Horses like nice weather. They are not _____ the cold weather of Antarctica.
3. Amundsen went to sea as a worker first. Then he _____ to be a captain.
4. Amundsen's ship was _____ to the Arctic when they found the Northwest Passage.

USE

Work with a partner to answer the questions. Use complete sentences.

1. What places in the world have *extreme* weather?
2. What kinds of *races* do you have in your country?
3. What kind of *fuel* do you use for heat? For a car? For lights?
4. What have you *already* done today?
5. What is one *goal* that you hope to reach in your life?
6. What kind of weather are you *used to*?

COMPREHENSION

UNDERSTANDING THE READING

Circle the letter of the correct answer.

1. Amundsen _____.
   a. always wanted to reach the South Pole
   b. was already famous before he reached the South Pole
   c. never wanted to go to the North Pole
   d. never wanted to be the captain of a ship

2. Amundsen _____.

   a. reached the South Pole after Scott

   b. reached the South Pole before Peary

   c. reached the South Pole before Scott

   d. reached the South Pole after Peary

3. Amundsen _____.

   a. found Nobile's airship after the crash

   b. died as he looked for his friend Nobile

   c. died with Nobile in the airship crash

   d. died after he found Nobile and the crashed airship

REMEMBERING DETAILS

Reread the passage and answer the questions.

1. Where did Amundsen's ship go in 1903?
2. What country did Robert Peary, the North Pole explorer, come from?
3. When did Amundsen reach the South Pole?
4. When did Scott reach the South Pole?
5. Where did they find the bodies of Scott and his men?
6. What did Amundsen and Nobile do together?

MAKING INFERENCES

All of the statements below are true. Some of them are stated directly in the reading. Others can be inferred, or guessed, from the reading. Write _S_ for each stated fact. Write _I_ for each inference.

_____ 1. Scott was not an experienced explorer like Amundsen.

_____ 2. Scott used horses to pull his sleds.

_____ 3. Scott and his men froze because they had no fuel for heat.

_____ 4. Future explorers learned a lot from Scott's death.

_____ 5. Amundsen was the first person to reach the South Pole and the first to fly over the North Pole.

TELL THE STORY

Work with a partner or together as a class. Tell the story of who reached the South Pole first. Use your own words. Your partner or other students can ask questions about the story.

DISCUSSION

Discuss the answers to these questions with your classmates.

1. Some people like to prepare to go on a trip, and some people do not. What preparations do you make before you go on a trip? Do you like preparing for a trip? Why or why not?

2. Why do people go on difficult and dangerous voyages? Would you like to go on a difficult or dangerous voyage? Why or why not?

3. Which would you prefer to visit: the North Pole, a tropical rainforest, or the Sahara Desert? Talk about your choice.

WRITING

Write six sentences or a short paragraph about the place you chose for Discussion question 3.

Example: *I would like to visit the Sahara Desert. I saw it in films, and it looks very beautiful.*

_____

_____

_____

_____

_____

_____

Spelling and Punctuation

COMMAS: BEFORE *AND*, *BUT*, AND *OR*

We use a comma before the words *and, but,* and *or* when they join two sentences together.

Amundsen was now a famous explorer. He started to plan his voyage to the North Pole.   (two sentences)

*Amundsen was now a famous explorer**, and** he started to plan his voyage to the North Pole.*   (*and* joins two sentences)

Scott and his men were on their way. They were not prepared for the extreme weather.   (two sentences)

*Scott and his men were on their way**, but** they were not prepared for the extreme weather.*   (*but* joins two sentences)

We do <u>not</u> use a comma before *and, but,* and *or* in a simple sentence. In a simple sentence *and, but,* and *or* join two nouns, two adjectives, two adverbs, or two verbs.

He had teams of dogs to pull sleds with <u>food</u> *and* <u>tents</u>.

They didn't <u>eat</u> *or* <u>sleep</u> *for days.*

Put commas in the correct places. Some sentences do not need commas.

1. Amundsen read about explorers going to the North Pole and he wanted to go there, too.

2. He worked on a boat that went to Antarctica but didn't go to the South Pole.

3. Amundsen gathered supplies and men.

4. They were tired but happy when they reached the South Pole.

5. There was snow and ice everywhere but the men weren't worried.

6. It was important for Amundsen to be the first to get to the North Pole or the South Pole.

7. Amundsen had dogs to pull the sleds but Scott had horses.

8. People had no news of Scott or his men.

UNIT 6

What Is the Royal Flying Doctor Service?

BEFORE YOU READ

Answer these questions.

1. If you are far from a city or town in your country, how do you get medical help?
2. Is it difficult to get medical help in an emergency?
3. What are some methods of communication and transportation that make it possible to get medical help quickly?

What Is the Royal Flying Doctor Service?

1 Most people in Australia live in cities on the coast. Very few people live in the huge middle area, and houses are far away from each other. Australians call this part of the country "the Outback." In the past, when people in the Outback **had an accident** or got sick, there were no doctors to take care of them. Today people in the Outback can call a special **service** called the Royal Flying Doctor Service and get help in a few minutes. The Royal Flying Doctors use airplanes to reach people in places that don't have doctors.

2 A **minister**, Reverend John Flynn, started the Flying Doctor Service in the 1920s. He traveled by **truck** through central and northern Australia for his church. Many times he saw people die because there was no doctor near. He thought, "There must be some way to help these people. First, I will build **hospitals** for them."

3 Flynn worked very hard, and by 1927 there were ten small hospitals in central and northern Australia. Nurses took care of the sick and **injured** people. But Flynn was not **satisfied**. He had hospitals and nurses, but he needed doctors. But how could doctors visit the people who lived far away in the Outback and could not go to a hospital? He had an idea! "The doctors can travel by airplane. We will also build a place for a plane to land near every Outback home." Many people laughed at the idea. Airplane travel in 1927 was a new and dangerous thing.

4 There were other problems, too. How can people so far away ask for a doctor? Flynn said, "We will use a radio to send and **receive** messages." At that time, radios in the Outback could receive messages, but they could not send them. Flynn **got in touch with** a young radio engineer. The engineer agreed to help him. The engineer worked for three years and finally made a radio that could send and receive messages.

5 Everything was ready. The Flying Doctor Service began in May 1928. The Service was a great success, and Flynn was very happy. In the first year, doctors made fifty flights. They flew 18,000 miles, helped 225 people, and saved 4 lives. Flynn now wanted the Service to be in all parts of the Outback. His church did not have enough money for this plan, so the different states in Australia agreed to help. Each state built one or two hospitals.

6 In 1942, the Flying Doctor Service **came up with** another good idea. Every home in the Outback got a prepared **first-aid kit**. Each kit had the same drugs, bandages, and other first-aid materials. Everything in the kit had its own special number. Later, the kits had a picture of a body with numbers for all the different parts. When people got sick or injured, they used the radio to call the medical center. The doctor asked about the problem by number. Then the doctor told the caller to use medicine from the kit by numbers, too. For example, the doctor said, "Take one **pill** from number 8 every three hours," or "Put number 22 on your injured leg."

7 Today there are 3,000 medical kits, 22 hospitals, and 40 Royal Flying Doctor Service airplanes. Each year, the service helps about 197,000 people.

VOCABULARY

MEANING

Write the correct words in the blanks.

satisfied	hospitals	injured	minister
truck	service	pills	receive

1. The Royal Flying Doctors is a special medical organization. It is a _____ that helps sick people in the Outback of Australia.
2. Reverend Flynn was a _____ in his church.
3. Flynn drove a _____ around the Outback and saw many sick people die.
4. He wanted to build _____ to help the sick.
5. Flynn had nurses to help him, but he was not _____. He needed doctors, too.
6. People went to the hospital for different reasons. Some were _____, and some were sick.
7. Flynn needed a radio to send and _____ messages.
8. The first-aid kits have bandages and different kinds of _____.

WORDS THAT GO TOGETHER

Write the correct words in the blanks.

got in touch with	had an accident	first-aid kit	came up with

1. In the past, when a person in the Outback _____, there wasn't a doctor to call.

2. Flynn heard about an engineer and _____ him. Flynn talked to him about making a special radio.

3. Flynn always _____ new ideas to improve the Service.

4. It is important to have a _____ at home to help when someone gets sick or injured.

USE

Work with a partner to answer the questions. Use complete sentences.

1. Why is it good to have a *first-aid kit*?

2. What is a *service* you use every day?

3. What should you do when someone *has an accident*?

4. How do you *get in touch with* your doctor?

5. Where do you take an *injured* person?

6. How many e-mails or phone calls do you *receive* every day?

COMPREHENSION

UNDERSTANDING THE READING

Circle the letter of the correct answer.

1. Reverend John Flynn _____.

    a. started the Flying Doctor Service

    b. was the first man to visit central and northern Australia

    c. was a doctor who started the Flying Doctor Service

    d. was a doctor who loved to fly

2. The Flying Doctor Service _____.

   a. was not a success in the beginning

   b. helps all people who can afford it

   c. used special radios and airplanes

   d. had no hospitals

3. Outback homes _____.

   a. have special phone numbers

   b. each have their own airplane

   c. have many hospitals nearby

   d. have special first-aid kits

REMEMBERING DETAILS

Circle *T* if the sentence is true. Circle *F* if the sentence is false.

1.	Flynn traveled for his church all over Australia.	**T**	**F**
2.	Flynn's first idea was to build hospitals.	**T**	**F**
3.	Flynn made a radio that could send and receive messages.	**T**	**F**
4.	Each first-aid kit has the same things in it.	**T**	**F**
5.	Everything in the kit has a letter of the alphabet on it.	**T**	**F**
6.	Today the Flying Doctor Service has 22 hospitals.	**T**	**F**

MAKING INFERENCES

All of the statements below are true. Some of them are stated directly in the reading. Others can be inferred, or guessed, from the reading. Write *S* for each stated fact. Write *I* for each inference.

____ 1. Today people use all types of technology to get in touch with the Service.

____ 2. The Service is still very useful and helps thousands of people every year.

____ 3. People who know little English can use the first-aid kit.

____ 4. Everything in the kit has numbers on it, so it is easy to use.

____ 5. It is very expensive to operate the Service.

Work with a partner or together as a class. Tell the story of the Royal Flying Doctor Service. Use your own words. Your partner or other students can ask questions about the story.

DISCUSSION

Discuss the answers to these questions with your classmates.

1. Would a service like the Royal Flying Doctors work well in your country? Why or why not?
2. What medical services do people need that your country does not have?
3. What can countries do to improve]medical services for people who don't live in cities?

WRITING

Write six sentences or a short paragraph about the medical service you use.

Example: *In my country, when I get sick, I call my doctor for an appointment.*

_____

_____

_____

_____

_____

_____

SPELLING AND PUNCTUATION

CAPITAL LETTERS: DIRECT QUOTATIONS

We begin the first word in a direct quotation with a capital letter. If the quotation is divided in two parts, begin the second part with a small letter. Only use a capital letter for the second part if it is a new sentence.

He said, "There must be some way to help these people. First, I will build hospitals for them."

"There must be some way," he said, "to help these people."

"There must be some way to help these people," he said. "First, I will build hospitals for them."

A. Write C for sentences with the correct capital letters. Rewrite the incorrect sentences.

1. Flynn said, "the doctors can travel by airplane!"

   _____

2. His friend asked, "how can they do that?"

   _____

3. Flynn answered, "we will build a place for a plane to land near every Outback home."

   _____

4. "That's impossible," his friend said, "but we can always try."

   _____

5. His friend asked, "how can people so far away ask for a doctor?"

   _____

6. Flynn said, "we will use a radio to send and receive messages."

   _____

7. "Radios can receive messages," his friend said, "but they cannot send them."

   _____

8. The doctor said, "take one pill from number 7 every three hours."

   _____

9. "Put number 16 on your arm," the doctor said, "And take one pill from number 8."

   _____

10. The doctor said, "call me back tomorrow at the same time, and tell me how you feel."

   _____

B. Write two sentences with direct quotations.

   _____

   _____

UNIT 7

How Did the Egyptians Make Mummies?

BEFORE YOU READ

Answer these questions.

1. What is a mummy?
2. Which countries have mummies?
3. Where can you see mummies today?

How Did the Egyptians Make Mummies?

1 The ancient Egyptians **believed in** many gods. They also believed that their kings, called pharaohs, were gods. They believed that the pharaoh could help them even after he died. Because of this, they wanted the pharaoh to have a good life, and a good life after death, or afterlife. One way to give the pharaoh a good afterlife was to **preserve** his body. Egyptians believed this was important for the pharoah's **spirit**. This would help the spirit **recognize** the body. This is the reason the Egyptians made mummies.

2 As soon as a pharaoh died, the top priest, together with his helpers, started work on the body. They took out some of the organs but left the heart inside the body. They dried the organs and put them in special jars. Later they put the jars in the pharaoh's tomb, a special building for the dead. Next they took out the brain and threw it away. The Egyptians did not think the brain was important. On the outside of the body, they rubbed a kind of salt on the skin to help dry the body completely. This took about forty days. Then they filled the body with cloth and sand to keep its shape, rubbed it with oil and perfumes, and covered it with lots of **wax**. The Arabic word for wax is *mum*, so that's how we got the word *mummy*.

3 The pharaoh's body was now prepared. Next they wrapped it in very long pieces of cloth. Again, they used a lot of wax to make the pieces stick together. **At last**, after seventy days, the mummy was ready. They painted the face of the dead pharaoh on the mummy to help his spirit recognize him. The mummy then went into two or three coffins, one inside the other, and finally into the tomb.

4 During his lifetime, a pharaoh also prepared for the afterlife. He built his tomb, which took many years and a lot of hard work. The tomb was **in the shape of** a pyramid. The pointed top helped the pharaoh's spirit climb into the sky to join the gods who lived there. Each pharaoh tried to be greater than the one before, so the pyramids got larger and larger. More than seventy pharaohs built pyramids for themselves. The Great Pyramid at Giza is still the largest stone structure in the world. The tomb was filled with everything the person needed for the afterlife, **such as**

(continued)

food, clothing, and jewelry. There were also model figures of men and women called *shabtis*. These figures became workers for the pharaoh in the afterlife. Some tombs had 365 shabtis, one for each day of the year.

5 Later other people such as priests, people in government, and rich Egyptians also wanted to be mummies so that they could join the pharaoh in the afterlife. They even made some animals such as cats, dogs, and birds into mummies because these animals represented gods.

6 When everything was in the tomb, they closed it very **tight**. Egyptians believed a pharaoh's tomb was like the house of a god. If someone entered it, terrible things would happen to that person—he or she could even die. But this did not stop people from entering the tombs. During construction, some workers built secret **tunnels** into the pyramids. Then they went in later to **steal** from them. Some coffins had special doors for the same reason. **Thieves** went into almost all the tombs. They stole **treasures** such as gold and jewelry.

7 Today, most of the treasures are lost or in museums, but the pyramids of Egypt are still there. Every year, thousands of tourists from around the world visit the pyramids and think of the pharaohs who built them. So in a way, the pharaohs reached their goal—they live on, at least through their tombs.

VOCABULARY

MEANING

Write the correct words in the blanks.

recognize	preserve	steal	treasures	wax
thieves	tunnels	tight	spirit	

1. Egyptians wanted to keep the body of the pharaoh in good condition after he died. They wanted to _____ the body.

2. The Egyptians believed that after a person died, his or her _____ was still alive.

3. The Egyptians used _____, a sticky substance made by bees, to make a mummy.

4. They painted the face of the dead person on the mummy to help his spirit _____ him.

5. They put everything in the tomb and closed it _____. They wanted the tombs to stay shut.

6. The tombs had _____ in them like gold and jewelry.

7. Some people wanted the gold and jewelry. They went into the tomb to _____ them.

8. _____ took gold and jewelry from the tombs.

9. They dug through the pyramids to make special roads and passages called _____.

WORDS THAT GO TOGETHER

Write the correct words in the blanks.

believed in	at last	in the shape of	such as

1. The ancient Egyptians _____ _____ many gods.

2. The pharaohs wanted their tombs to look like pyramids. They built the tombs _____ pyramids.

3. It took a long time to clean, dry, and wrap the dead body. _____ _____ , after seventy days, the mummy was ready.

4. The Egyptians did many things to the dead body, _____ filling it with sand, rubbing it with oil, and covering it with wax.

USE

Work with a partner to answer the questions. Use complete sentences.

1. What do we use *wax* for today?
2. How can you *preserve* food?
3. Where do we usually find *tunnels*?
4. How do you *recognize* your house or apartment from the others near it?
5. Do you have any *treasures*? What are they?
6. What kinds of jewelry do you like? Give examples with *such as*.
7. Did someone ever *steal* something from you? What was it?

COMPREHENSION

UNDERSTANDING THE READING

Circle the letter of the correct answer.

1. The ancient Egyptians believed in _____.
   a. pharaohs
   b. life after death
   c. mummies
   d. tombs

2. Workers started to build a tomb for a pharaoh _____.
   a. during the pharaoh's lifetime
   b. after the pharaoh died
   c. when the pharaoh was old
   d. when a pharaoh was born

3. Thieves stole the _____ from most of the pyramids in Egypt.
   a. mummies
   b. treasures
   c. tombs
   d. shabits

REMEMBERING DETAILS

Reread the passage and answer the questions.

1. Who usually made the pharaoh's mummy?
2. What organ did they leave in the body?
3. Where did they put the special jars with the organs in them?
4. How long did it take to make a mummy?
5. Why was the tomb of a pharaoh in the shape of a pyramid?
6. How many pharaohs built pyramids?
7. Why did they put *shabtis* in the tomb?

MAKING INFERENCES

All of the statements below are true. Some of them are stated directly in the reading. Others can be inferred, or guessed, from the reading. Write *S* for each stated fact. Write *I* for each inference.

_____ 1. When an ordinary woman died, they did not make her into a mummy.

_____ 2. The top priest and his helpers made the pharaoh's mummy.

_____ 3. The tomb was in the shape of a pyramid so the pharoah's spirit could climb to the gods in the sky.

_____ 4. The Egyptians thought the heart was a very important organ.

_____ 5. A cat or dog was higher than an ordinary person.

TELL THE STORY

Work with a partner or together as a class. Tell the story of how the ancient Egyptians made mummies. Use your own words. Your partner or other students can ask questions about the story.

DISCUSSION

Discuss the answers to these questions with your classmates.

1. In some countries, people can pay a company to freeze their bodies after they die. They hope that people in the future can bring them back to life. What do you think about this?

2. Why do you think the Egyptians stopped building pyramids?

3. Should mummies be in museums for people to look at? Does this show respect to the dead people and their culture? Explain.

WRITING

Write six sentences or a short paragraph. Describe how you or your family prepares for a special event.

Example: *One month before the New Year, my mother begins to prepare the house for the New Year's celebration.*

_____

_____

_____

_____

_____

_____

SPELLING AND PUNCTUATION

EI OR *IE*?

Here is the general rule for using *ei* or *ie*:

Use *i* before *e*
Except after *c*
Or when sounded like *a*
As in n*ei*ghbor or w*ei*gh

We use *i* before *e*.

*The pr*ie*st started to work on the body.*

We use *ei* after *c*.

*The priest rec*ei*ved money from the rich.*

We use *ei* when it sounds like *a*.

*Each block of stone of a pyramid w*ei*ghed tons.*

There are exceptions to the rule! Here are some exceptions.

ancient   foreign   science   neither   their   leisure

A. Circle the correctly spelled words.

1. The pyramids of Egypt are (anceint/ancient).
2. There are wall paintings in the tombs of people working in the (feilds/fields).
3. The paintings also show people relaxing with (friends/freinds).
4. The Egyptians (beleived/believed) in life after death.
5. After a pharaoh (deid/died) they preserved the body.
6. They prepared (their/thier) tombs for the afterlife.
7. A pharaoh could marry a sister or a (neice/niece).
8. They (dreid/dried) the organs and put them in special jars.
9. They wrapped the body in long (peices/pieces) of cloth.
10. Did the Egyptians know about (science/sceince) at that time?
11. Did the Egyptians put (viels/veils) in the tombs?
12. Pyramids do not have a (cieling/ceiling) like a house has.

B. Write three sentences with *ei* or *ie* words.

_____

_____

_____

UNIT 8

Why Is Louis Pasteur Important?

BEFORE YOU READ

Answer these questions.

1. Who are some famous scientists?
2. Why do some scientists study diseases and germs?
3. Why are there fewer diseases today than there were hundreds of years ago?

Why Is Louis Pasteur Important?

1 Louis Pasteur was one of the first people to discover that diseases come from germs. The word *pasteurize* that we usually see on milk containers comes from his name.

2 Louis Pasteur was born in 1822 in a small village in France. As a boy, Louis **was interested in** art and was a very good painter. His father did not want his son to be an artist when he grew up. He wanted Louis to be a great teacher. Louis was also interested in chemistry and other **sciences**, so he agreed with his father and decided to go to college.

3 After college, Louis attended a famous school in Paris that trains teachers, the École Normale Supérieure. He entered the school in 1843 to study how to teach chemistry and physics. He soon **made a name for himself** with his research. After he graduated, he became a professor at the University of Strasbourg. At the university, he met Marie Laurent, the daughter of the director of the university. They **fell in love** and married in 1849. They were very happy and had five children. Sadly, only one boy and one girl lived to be adults.

4 In 1854, Louis took a job at the University of Lille, a city in the north of France. He was a professor of chemistry and dean of the faculty of science—a very high position for a man of thirty-two. Around this time, the French wine industry was in terrible **trouble**. Their wine was sour and they didn't know why. The winemakers around Lille asked Pasteur to help them. After many experiments, Louis discovered that the problem came from germs. The **solution** was to heat the wine. This would kill the **harmful** germs. The winemakers were shocked, but the method worked. Soon they also heated other drinks such as beer and milk. This made them safe to drink. The method was called pasteurization, after Louis Pasteur.

5 In 1857, Pasteur returned to Paris to become director of science studies at the École Normale Supérieure. At that time, there was a terrible disease called anthrax. It killed thousands of sheep and cows every year. Pasteur **noticed** something interesting. If an animal was sick with anthrax and **got well**, it never caught the disease again. He decided to inject healthy sheep with **weak** anthrax germs. These sheep lived and never caught the disease. Pasteur had a vaccine against anthrax!

(continued)

6 One day in 1885, a doctor brought a nine-year-old boy named Joseph Meister to Pasteur. A mad dog with the disease rabies bit the boy, and the doctor didn't know how to save him. In the past, Pasteur helped animals with this disease, but would his method work on humans, or would the boy die? Pasteur was very **worried**, but finally he tried an experiment. He injected Joseph with his vaccine and sat by his bed to watch the result. The boy lived! Immediately the news spread around the world, and Pasteur was famous.

7 Pasteur wanted to build a research institute in Paris to continue his work. People read about his methods and sent money from all over the world to help build the institute. The Pasteur Institute opened its doors in 1888. It is still one of the world's most respected centers for the study of diseases and how to fight them. Pasteur was the director of the Institute and he worked there until he died in 1895. Everyone remembered Pasteur as a great man.

8 Years later, during World War II, the Germans came to Paris. A German officer wanted to open Pasteur's tomb, but the old French guard said no. When the German demanded that he open it or die, the guard killed himself. The name of the guard was Joseph Meister.

VOCABULARY

MEANING

Write the correct words in the blanks.

noticed	sciences	worried	solution
harmful	weak	sour	trouble

1. Louis Pasteur liked art, but he also liked the _____, such as physics and chemistry.

2. When wine becomes bad and people can't drink it, it tastes _____ like vinegar.

3. Pasteur had to find a _____ to the winemakers' problem.

4. The winemakers had problems and needed help. The French wine industry was in _____.

5. We can kill dangerous and _____ germs with heat.

6. Pasteur _____ that if an animal with anthrax becomes healthy, it never catches the disease again.

7. He injected sheep with anthrax germs. These germs were not strong. They were _____.

8. Pasteur was _____ about Joseph. The little boy needed help, but Louis didn't want to hurt him.

WORDS THAT GO TOGETHER

Write the correct words in the blanks.

| got well | was interested in | fell in love | made a name for himself |

1. Pasteur liked to paint and draw pictures. He _____ art.

2. People began to know about Pasteur because he did important research. Pasteur _____ in the world of science.

3. Pasteur _____ with Marie Laurent, and they got married in 1849.

4. Animals that were sick with anthrax and _____ never had the disease again.

USE

Work with a partner to answer the questions. Use complete sentences.

1. What is something that is *harmful* to people?

2. What foods or drinks have a *sour* taste? Do you like how they taste?

3. What do you *worry* about?

4. Do you ever feel weak? What are some other things that are or can be weak? (for example, a sick person, coffee)

5. What subjects *are* you *interested in*?

6. Did you ever *fall in love* with someone? Who? What happened?

7. When you catch a cold, what do you do to *get well*?

COMPREHENSION

UNDERSTANDING THE READING

Circle the letter of the correct answer.

1. Louis Pasteur discovered _____.
   a. how to make wine and beer
   b. a way to kill harmful germs
   c. how to make a better wine
   d. a way to make wine taste sour

2. Pasteur _____.
   a. invented a vaccine for anthrax and other diseases
   b. invented a method to pasteurize sheep
   c. discovered a new disease
   d. invented vaccines for animals but not humans

3. Pasteur's research institute _____.
   a. closed because of World War II
   b. is a museum today
   c. continues to operate today
   d. closed when Pasteur died in 1895

REMEMBERING DETAILS

Reread the passage and fill in the blanks.

1. Marie Laurent was the daughter of the director of the _____.
2. Louis and Marie Pasteur had _____ children.
3. Pasteur's solution was _____ the sour wine. This killed the germs.
4. Before the vaccine, anthrax killed _____ every year.
5. Louis didn't know whether his rabies vaccine worked _____. He was worried, but he gave it to Joseph Meister and waited for the result.
6. The Pasteur Institute is a research center for the study of _____.

MAKING INFERENCES

All of the statements below are true. Some of them are stated directly in the reading. Others can be inferred, or guessed, from the reading. Write *S* for each stated fact. Write *I* for each inference.

_____ 1.   Pasteur was famous when he was alive.

_____ 2.   It worried Pasteur to experiment on Joseph Meister because Pasteur was not a doctor.

_____ 3.   Pasteur was not sure that his vaccine would work on humans.

_____ 4.   Joseph Meister worked at the Pasteur Institute because he wanted to be near the man who saved his life.

_____ 5.   Joseph Meister killed himself to save Pasteur's tomb.

TELL THE STORY

Work with a partner or together as a class. Tell the story of Louis Pasteur. Use your own words. Your partner or other students can ask questions about the story.

DISCUSSION

Discuss the answers to these questions with your classmates.

1.   What scientific discoveries have been made recently?
2.   Are all new medical discoveries good? Why or why not?
3.   How safe are vaccines and medicines? What about natural remedies, such as herbs and vitamins?

WRITING

Write six sentences or a short paragraph about a medical discovery that has helped people.

Example: *I think antibiotics were a great discovery. Before we had antibiotics many people died.*

_____

_____

_____

_____

_____

_____

SPELLING AND PUNCTUATION

QUESTION MARKS

> We use a question mark at the end of a question. The question can be a direct question, a tag question, or a polite request.
>
> Direct question   *Would the boy die?*
>
> Tag question   *The story of Louis Pasteur is interesting, isn't it?*
>
> Polite request   *Could you help me with my report about Louis Pasteur?*

A. Write *C* for sentences with correct punctuation. Rewrite the incorrect sentences.

1. Have you seen a rabid dog.

   _____

2. Did you know that the word *pasteurization* comes from Pasteur's name.

   _____

3. Pasteurization is an amazing discovery.

   _____

4. Do you know that some animals catch anthrax and others do not?

   _____

B. Add the correct end punctuation to the sentences. You can use question marks or periods.

1. Why was the wine going bad

2. Do you think the idea would work on humans

3. Could you explain how wine is pasteurized

4. Is it true that Pasteur found the cure for anthrax

5. When people are vaccinated against a disease, they don't catch it

6. Rabies can kill you, can't it

7. They didn't know why the wine was getting sour

8. The Pasteur Institute is in Paris

UNIT 9

Who Is Nasreddin Hodja?

BEFORE YOU READ

Answer these questions.

1. Do you like to tell or to hear funny stories?
2. Who are some comedians in your country? Do you think people in other countries would like them, too?
3. Folk stories are stories that parents tell children about people or events from history. These stories are not completely true, but children enjoy them and sometimes learn from them. What folk stories do you know?

Who Is Nasreddin Hodja?

1 Everybody in Turkey knows the stories about Nasreddin Hodja. These funny stories are part of Turkish folk culture. Nasreddin Hodja was a man who lived near Ankara, in central Turkey, **in the thirteenth century**. The jokes and stories are about Nasreddin's daily life. Some of these stories are about eight hundred years old, and they are still funny. Here are some Nasreddin Hodja stories.

The Pot That Gave Birth

2 Nasreddin Hodja borrowed a large pot from his **neighbor**. Days and weeks passed, but he didn't return the pot. One day the neighbor came over and asked to have his pot back. Hodja **apologized**, "I am sorry. I forgot to return it. But," he said, "I have good news for you. While the pot was at my house, it **gave birth to** a smaller pot."

3 Hodja handed his neighbor the big pot and the "baby" pot, and the neighbor went home happily with two pots.

4 A few weeks later, Hodja **knocked** on his neighbor's door and asked to borrow the large pot again. The neighbor remembered the good experience from the first time, so he was happy to lend his pot to Hodja again.

5 Weeks passed and there was **no word from** Hodja about the pot. The neighbor decided to go to Hodja's house, as before, and ask him to return the pot. When Hodja opened the door, the neighbor asked to have the pot back. Hodja, with a sad face, told the man that the large pot died.

6 The neighbor was shocked and angry and said, "What do you think I am, an idiot? Do you want me to believe that a pot died?"

7 "My good man," Hodja replied with a smile, "you had no trouble believing that a pot gave birth."

Tiger Powder

8 One day Nasreddin Hodja was outside. His neighbor saw Hodja putting some powder on the ground around his house. The neighbor asked, "Hodja, what are you doing?"

9 Hodja replied, "I want to keep the tigers away."

10 The neighbor said, "But there are no tigers within hundreds of miles."

11 "**Effective**, isn't it?" Hodja replied.

The Opinions of Men

12 Hodja and his son went on a journey to another town. They only had one donkey. Hodja told his son to ride the donkey. Hodja preferred to walk. On the way, they met some people who said, "Look at that healthy boy! That's today's **youth**. They **have** no **respect for** their elders. He is riding on the donkey and his **poor** father is walking!"

13 When they passed these people, the boy felt bad. He told his father to ride the donkey while he walked. So Hodja rode the donkey, and the boy walked at his side.

14 A little later, they met other people who said, "Well, look at that! That poor boy has to walk while his father is riding the donkey."

15 After they passed these people, Hodja told his son, "The best thing is for both of us to walk. Then, no one can **complain**." So they continued their journey on foot, walking beside the donkey.

16 Down the road, they met some others who said, "Just look at those idiots. Both of them are walking under this hot sun and neither of them is riding the donkey!"

17 Hodja turned to his son and said, "That shows you how hard it is to **escape** the opinions of men."

Backward Donkey

18 One day, Nasreddin Hodja got on his donkey the wrong way, facing backward.

19 "Hodja," the people said, "you are sitting on your donkey backward!"

20 "No," he replied. "I am sitting on the donkey correctly. It is the donkey that is facing backward."

21 The stories of Nasreddin Hodja are now in many languages. They are popular all over the world. In honor of Nasreddin Hodja, UNESCO (The United Nations Education, Scientific, and Cultural Organization) decided to call 1996–1997 International Nasreddin Hodja Year.

VOCABULARY

MEANING

Write the correct words in the blanks.

apologized	complain	effective	knocked
escape	neighbor	poor	youth

1. Nasreddin Hodja borrowed a pot from a man who lived near him. He borrowed from his _____.

2. Nasreddin said he was sorry. He _____.

3. Nasreddin _____ on the door. He wanted the man inside to know he was there.

4. The tiger powder worked very well. It was _____.

5. The young people of today, or today's _____, do not respect older people.

6. When you pity a man or think he is not lucky, you say, "_____ man!"

7. People like to talk about why they are not happy. They like to _____.

8. Nasreddin and his son could not get away from the bad opinions of others. They couldn't _____ from them.

WORDS THAT GO TOGETHER

Write the correct words in the blanks.

have respect for	in the thirteenth century
gave birth to	no word from

1. Nasreddin Hodja lived in the 1200s. He lived _____.

2. The people on the road said today's youth don't admire, or _____, their elders.

3. Hodja's neighbor could not believe a baby pot came from another pot. But Hodja said the pot _____ the baby.

4. Hodja didn't see or talk to his neighbor for a long time. There was _____ from Hodja.

Work with a partner to answer the questions. Use complete sentences.

1. Who is a famous person who lived *in the twentieth century*?
2. What is your *neighbor* like? Are you friends?
3. What kind of music does today's *youth* listen to?
4. What people do you *have respect for*?

COMPREHENSION

UNDERSTANDING THE READING

Circle the letter of the correct answer.

1. Nasreddin Hodja's stories are _____.
   a. about 800 years old
   b. about his job and co-workers
   c. not funny
   d. from English folk culture

2. In the story "The Pot That Gave Birth," Hodja _____.
   a. gave back one pot the first time
   b. didn't give back the pot the second time
   c. gave two pots back the second time
   d. didn't give anything back the first time

3. In the story "The Opinions of Men," people criticized Hodja _____.
   a. because he went to another town
   b. because the boy was bad
   c. when he and his son sat on the donkey
   d. no matter what he did (in every situation)

REMEMBERING DETAILS

Circle *T* if the sentence is true. Circle *F* if the sentence is false.

1.	Nasreddin Hodja lived near Ankara, Turkey.	T	F
2.	Hodja sat on his donkey the wrong way.	T	F
3.	Nasreddin Hodja stories are only in Turkish.	T	F
4.	Hodja and his son went to another country on a donkey.	T	F

5. Hodja and his son were walking in the rain and   T   F
neither one was riding the donkey.

6. Hodja didn't return the pot to his neighbor for weeks.   T   F

MAKING INFERENCES

All of the statements below are true. Some of them are stated directly in the reading. Others can be inferred, or guessed, from the reading. Write *S* for each stated fact. Write *I* for each inference.

_____ 1. The neighbor was happy to lend him the pot a second time.

_____ 2. The usual animal in Hodja stories is the donkey.

_____ 3. People in Turkey today still tell Hodja stories.

_____ 4. Hodja said that people will criticize you in any situation.

_____ 5. The United Nations honored Nasreddin Hodja in 1996.

TELL THE STORY

Work with a partner or together as a class. Tell one of Nasreddin Hodja's stories. Use your own words. Your partner or other students can ask questions about the story.

DISCUSSION

Discuss the answers to these questions with your classmates.

1. What do you think of Nasreddin Hodja's stories?

2. What lesson did you learn from "The Pot That Gave Birth"?

3. What stories from your country are like Nasreddin Hodja stories? Tell one.

WRITING

Write six sentences or a short paragraph about something funny that happened to you or a person you know.

Example: *Last year, my grandmother visited me in my apartment. My grandmother didn't know how the answering machine worked . . .*

_____

_____

_____

_____

_____

_____

SPELLING AND PUNCTUATION

QUOTATION MARKS: DIRECT QUOTATIONS

A direct quotation repeats the exact words a person said. We use quotation marks at the beginning and at the end of each part of a direct quotation. We put punctuation inside the second quotation mark.

Hodja said, "I am sorry. I forgot to return it."

We do not use quotation marks in reported speech. Reported speech does not use a person's exact words.

The neighbor asked to have his pot back.

Write *C* for sentences with correct punctuation. Rewrite the incorrect sentences. Don't forget to capitalize the first word in a direct quotation (see Unit 6).

1. Hodja said that he wanted to keep the tigers away.

   _____

2. One man said, what a healthy boy!

   _____

3. Hodja said the pot has passed away.

   _____

4. The neighbor said that he didn't believe him.

   _____

5. Hodja said I have good news for you.

   _____

6. What do you think I am? said the neighbor, Do you want me to believe that a pot died?

   _____

7. Look! He's riding on a donkey! Some people said, and his father is walking.

   _____

8. Hodja told his son that the best thing to do was walk.

   _____

9. He said then no one can complain.

   _____

10. That shows Hodja said, how hard it is to escape the opinions of men.

   _____

SELF-TEST 1
Units 1–9

A. SENTENCE COMPLETION

Circle the letter of the correct answer.

1. Gutenberg _____ in history.
   a. was the importantest man
   b. was the most important man
   c. the most important man was
   d. was most important man

2. If _____, they think she is healthy.
   a. a woman is fat
   b. woman was fat
   c. a woman will be fat
   d. fat is a woman

3. Each doll _____ on the steps.
   a. have its place
   b. have their place
   c. has its place
   d. has it's place

4. Marco Polo knew _____.
   a. no one believed himself
   b. no one believed him
   c. anybody believed him
   d. no one him believed

5. They waited for months, but _____ of Scott and his men.
   a. there were no news
   b. there weren't any news
   c. there was any news
   d. there was no news

6. At that time, radios in the Outback could receive messages, _____ they could not send them.
   a. and
   b. or
   c. but
   d. so

7. If someone entered a pharaoh's tomb, _____ to that person.
   a. terrible things could happen
   b. terrible things will happen
   c. things terrible could happen
   d. terrible things happen

8. The word *pasteurize* _____ on milk containers comes from Pasteur's name.
   a. who we usually see
   c. that usually we see
   b. that we usually see
   d. that usually see

9. Nasreddin Hodja's stories _____.
   a. are funny today still
   c. were still funny today
   b. are still funny today
   d. have still funny today

B. VOCABULARY

Complete the definitions. Circle the letter of the correct answer.

1. There weren't many books before the printing press. Books were _____.
   a. huge
   b. rare
   c. broke
   d. over

2. In Niger, women want to be as fat as possible so they eat _____ amounts of food.
   a. slim
   b. enough
   c. enormous
   d. responsible

3. The dolls have clothes and look like the ancient royal family in Japan. They _____ the royal family.
   a. represent
   b. arrange
   c. borrow
   d. give up

4. Marco Polo could not stay in one place for long when he returned from China. He couldn't _____.
   a. pass the time
   b. settle down
   c. pass through
   d. look like

5. Amundsen could not see Scott anywhere. There was _____ Scott.
   a. no sign of
   b. no word from
   c. had no idea
   d. on his way

6. In an accident, a person may be _____ and hurt.
   a. preserved
   b. noticed
   c. injured
   d. satisfied

7. Thieves went into the tombs and stole expensive old pieces of gold and jewelry. They stole _____.

    a. swords   b. pills   c. costumes   d. treasures

8. Some germs are _____ and can may you sick.

    a. weak   b. harmful   c. sour   d. tight

9. Nasreddin Hodja forgot to return the pot, so he said he was sorry and _____.

    a. knocked   b. apologized   c. complained   d. escaped

C. SPELLING AND PUNCTUATION

Circle the letter of the sentence with the correct spelling and punctuation.

1. a. Only the rich new how to read and write.
   b. Only the rich knew how to read and write.
   c. Only the rich knew how to read and right.
   d. Only the rich knew how to wread and write.

2. a. She hopped running would make her slimmer.
   b. She hoped runing would make her slimmer.
   c. She hoped running would make her slimer.
   d. She hoped running would make her slimmer.

3. a. Grandparents give their granddaughter a set of dolls.
   b. Grandparents give they're granddaughter a set of dolls.
   c. Grandparents give theire granddaughter a set of dolls.
   d. Granparents give there granddaughter a set of dolls.

4. a. Marco Polo traveled to China with his Father and Uncle.
   b. Marco Polo traveled to China with his Father and uncle.
   c. Marco Polo traveled to China with his father and Uncle.
   d. Marco Polo traveled to China with his father and uncle.

5. a. Amundsen was on a boat that went to, Antarctica but he didn't go to the South Pole.

   b. Amundsen was on a boat that went to Antarctica but he didn't go to the South Pole.

   c. Amundsen was on a boat that went to Antarctica but, he didn't go to the South Pole.

   d. Amundsen was on a boat that went to Antarctica, but he didn't go to the South Pole.

6. a. "Take one pill from number 8, the doctor said, "and call me in the morning."

   b. "Take one pill from number 8, "the doctor said, "and call me in the morning."

   c. "Take one pill from number 8," the doctor said, "and call me in the morning."

   d. "Take one pill from number 8," the doctor said, And call me in the morning."

7. a. The ancient Egyptians beleived there was life after they died.

   b. The anceint Egyptians belicved there was life after they died.

   c. The ancient Egyptians believed there was life after they died.

   d. The ancient Egyptians believed there was life after they deid.

8. a. Did he know why the wine was getting sour?.

   b. Did he know why the wine was getting sour.

   c. Did he know why the wine was getting sour?

   d. Did he know why the wine was getting sour

9. a. "The neighbor said, "I don't believe you."

   b. The neighbor said, "I don't believe you."

   c. "The neighbor said, I don't believe you."

   d. The neighbor said, I don't believe you.

UNIT 10

What Did the Ancient Mayans Believe In?

Answer these questions.

1. Where did the Mayans live?
2. What do you know about the Mayans' lives?
3. Do the Mayans exist today? If so, where?

What Did the Ancient Mayans Believe In?

1 The Mayan people of Mexico and Central America had the greatest **civilization** in the New World. The **height** of Mayan civilization was between 250 and 900. At this time, there were about fourteen million Maya. In forty of their cities, they built huge pyramids that were twenty-two stories high. Why did they build these pyramids? How did the Maya create their civilization? How did they structure their lives and society? Their beliefs guided them.

2 The Maya believed in time and numbers. They had a great knowledge of mathematics. They invented a number system that used only three symbols, and they invented zero. What would mathematics be without zero? They also made a calendar 2,600 years ago that was very **accurate**. It had 365 days in a year. There were three kinds of days on their calendar: good, bad, and **neutral**. People did important things on good or neutral days. They went on a journey, **got married**, or planted corn only on a good day. Time had a beginning and an end, too. They believed the world was going to end in 2012.

3 The Maya also believed in astrology; they believed that you could find all truth in the movement of the stars, the sun, and the moon. Astrology controlled their lives and their culture. The priests **predicted** the future by astrology. They did not have telescopes, but they knew all about the sky. The priests were called "He who knows" and were very important. They wore jewels and special feathers. People carried the priests on their shoulders in the streets. Everyone listened to the priests and believed in their predictions.

4 As soon as a baby was born, parents took it to the priest. The priest told the parents about the child's **destiny**. Each day on the Mayan calendar says what a baby born on that day will become. Parents had to **bring up** the child to be a farmer, a poet, a dancer, or another job the priest predicted. Each person lived **according to** his or her destiny.

5 The priests studied the sky to collect information, then they wrote their predictions in books. The Maya invented a writing system that used picture symbols. This was the first writing system in the Americas. They used tree bark for paper and made many books. Only a few books

(continued)

survive. We found a few of these books, but nobody could understand the writing. About fifty years ago, a researcher finally uncovered the meaning of the symbols. That is how we know about Mayan beliefs and predictions.

6 The Maya believed in many gods: the sun god, the moon god, and many other gods from nature. But the corn god was the most important. Without corn, they had no food. They believed all people came from the corn god. When a child was born, they put the head of the baby between two pieces of wood for several days. The shape of the baby's head became **permanently** flat and long. They thought this long, flat head looked like corn, which **was a sign of** high class. They also hung a small ball or bead from the baby's hair so that it fell between the baby's eyes. The child looked at this ball and later became cross-eyed. This was also a sign of beauty and high class.

7 Around the year 900, the Maya disappeared. We do not know what happened. Later, the Spanish came to their land and destroyed what was left of the Mayan culture, **including** most of the books filled with their predictions. The **descendants** of the Mayan people still exist in Mexico and other countries of Central America, such as El Salvador, Guatemala, and Belize. There are still Mayan priests among them, and they still use the old Mayan calendar to make predictions.

VOCABULARY

MEANING

What is the meaning of the underlined words? Circle the letter of the correct answer.

1. The <u>height</u> of Mayan civilization was between 250 and 900.
   a. center
   b. longest
   c. best
   d. worst

2. The Mayan people had the greatest <u>civilization</u> in the New World.
   a. the highest government official
   b. way of religious life
   c. a way of life, including laws, culture, and education
   d. style of buildings

3. They made a calendar that was very <u>accurate</u>.
   a. exact
   b. mysterious
   c. long
   d. changeable

4. They had priests who <u>predicted</u> the future.
   a. worried about
   b. said what was going to happen
   c. did not know much about
   d. made plans about

5. They had good, bad, and <u>neutral</u> days on their calendar.
   a. black
   b. especially good
   c. not bad or good
   d. dangerous

6. The priest told the parents the child's <u>destiny</u>.
   a. intelligence
   b. character
   c. future
   d. dreams

7. The baby's head became <u>permanently</u> flat and long.
   a. forever
   b. for a few months
   c. for a moment
   d. for a few years

8. The Spanish destroyed their culture, <u>including</u> their books
   a. part of which
   b. not together
   c. except for
   d. with information on

9. The <u>descendants</u> of the Mayan people live in Mexico and other countries of Central America.
   a. old friends from long ago
   b. priests and politicians
   c. people who study history
   d. people related to people who lived long ago

WORDS THAT GO TOGETHER

What is the meaning of the underlined words? Circle the letter of the correct answer.

1. A long, flat head was <u>a sign of</u> high class.
   a. an action of
   b. a symbol of
   c. a warning of
   d. a right of

2. Each person lived <u>according to</u> his or her destiny.

   a. in keeping with
   c. ahead of

   b. different from
   d. alone with

3. Parents had to <u>bring up</u> the child into something the priest predicted.

   a. raise
   c. have fun with

   b. talk about
   d. get happiness from

4. People <u>got married</u> or planted corn on a good day.

   a. when a man and woman became husband and wife
   c. when a man and a woman saw each other for the first time

   b. when a man and a woman fell in love
   d. when a man and a woman had children

USE

Work with a partner to answer the questions. Use complete sentences.

1. What kind of weather is *predicted* for tomorrow?
2. What is a *neutral* color?
3. Where were you *brought up*?
4. Where do you want to live *permanently*?
5. *According to* your teacher, what is the best way to learn new words?

COMPREHENSION

UNDERSTANDING THE READING

Circle the letter of the correct answer.

1. The Mayans believed _____.

   a. the world would never end
   c. some of the priests' predictions

   b. in time and numbers
   d. they should plant corn every day

2. The Mayans invented _____.

   a. the first writing system in the world
   c. a number system with 365 numbers

   b. the first writing system in the Americas
   d. the number system we use today

3. The Mayans _____.
   a. disappeared and have no descendants today
   b. disappeared but have descendants
   c. only live in Mexico today
   d. are Spanish today

REMEMBERING DETAILS

Reread the passage and answer the questions.

1. How tall were the Mayan pyramids?
2. How many kinds of days did they have on their calendar?
3. When did they believe the world will end?
4. Where did they believe all people came from?
5. What shape head did they think was a sign of high class?
6. Who destroyed what was left of the Mayan culture?
7. Where do descendants of the Mayans live today?

MAKING INFERENCES

All of the statements below are true. Some of them are stated directly in the reading. Others can be inferred, or guessed, from the reading. Write S for each stated fact. Write I for each inference.

_____ 1. The Spanish did not believe in the Mayans' ideas.

_____ 2. The Mayans had paper and books.

_____ 3. The Mayans believed that the world would end on a certain date.

_____ 4. The Mayans ate corn in some form with every meal.

_____ 5. Priests told the Mayans their destiny.

TELL THE STORY

Work with a partner or together as a class. Tell the story of the ancient Mayans. Use your own words. Your partner or other students can ask questions about the story.

DISCUSSION

Discuss the answers to these questions with your classmates.

1. What do you think happened to the Mayans?
2. What do you think about the Mayans' way of life? How do you think the Mayans would like society today? Explain.
3. Do you believe in predictions? Why or why not?

WRITING

Do you believe in astrology? Do you believe in luck? Write six sentences or a paragraph.

Example: *I believe in astrology and look at my horoscope. My sign is Virgo.*

_____

_____

_____

_____

_____

_____

SPELLING AND PUNCTUATION

NUMBERS AS WORDS

We usually spell out numbers of one or two words. We use figures for numbers that are more than two words.

*In **forty** of their cities, they built huge pyramids.*

*Their calendar had **365** days in a year.*

We spell all numbers that begin a sentence. You can also rewrite the sentence.

***Two thousand six hundred** years ago, they made a calendar.*

<u>or</u>

*They made a calendar **2,600** years ago.*

<u>not</u> *2,600 years ago, they made a calendar.*

We spell out the time in words when we use *o'clock*. We use numbers with A.M. **or** P.M.

*They got up at **five o'clock**.*

*His telephone rang at **5:15** A.M.*

Exceptions: In technical and business writing we sometimes use figures.

We usually use figures for:

Dates	*2012*	*July 4, 1776*
Addresses	*780 Bond Drive*	*402 West 49th Street*
Money	*$1.25*	*$916.95*

Write *C* for correct sentences. Rewrite the incorrect sentences with numbers.

1. 50 years ago, a researcher uncovered the meaning of the symbols used in Mayan writing.

   _____

2. The Mayans had a special date that came every 260 years.

   _____

3. The next date will be May 30, 2052.

   _____

4. They went to see the priest at 9 o'clock the next morning.

   _____

5. After 2 days, the child's head was flat.

   _____

6. They believe the world will end on December 12, 2012.

   _____

7. Their calendar had 18 months of 20 days each.

   _____

8. They had 5 days left over every year, and these days were very unlucky.

   _____

9. In 1572, a Spanish priest wrote that he had found 27 of their books and burnt them.

   _____

10. I was 4 years old when I went to El Salvador and met a man who was a descendant of the Mayans.

    _____

UNIT 11

How Do Koreans Celebrate a Wedding?

BEFORE YOU READ

Answer these questions.

1. What gifts do you give for an engagement or a wedding?
2. Do you prefer a modern or a traditional wedding?
3. What do you do after a wedding ceremony?

How Do Koreans Celebrate a Wedding?

1 In the past, parents in Korea arranged marriages for their children. Usually, they **hired** a matchmaker to help them. A matchmaker was usually a woman in the village. People paid her to find a good **match** for their son or daughter. The couple usually did not meet each other until the day of the wedding.

2 Today there are two ways to get married in Korea. The first is by a love match: two people meet, fall in love, and get married. There is no need for a third person. The second way is an arranged marriage: a third person chooses two people to marry each other, and if the two families agree, the next step is to visit the fortune-teller.

3 Koreans believe in the "four pillars." These are the year, month, day, and hour of a person's birth. A fortune-teller uses these four things to predict your destiny. Before a couple gets married, the fortune-teller looks at their four pillars to see whether they can be happy together. If the four pillars are bad for the couple, the family returns to the matchmaker to try again. If the four pillars are good for the couple, they can **get engaged**.

4 At the engagement **ceremony**, the two families get together. They can meet at the girl's house, a hotel, or a restaurant, but never at the boy's house. Today, families usually meet in a restaurant to **set a date** for the wedding. They always give each other lots of gifts. The two young people also **exchange** gifts. Some Korean families spend $30,000 to $40,000 on engagement gifts. One of the gifts to the girl's family is a special **document**. In the middle of a piece of expensive paper, her husband's four pillars are written in ink. The girl keeps this document all her life.

5 The time before the marriage ceremony is very exciting for the boy, called the groom, and the girl, called the bride. The groom's family sends a box of gifts (called a *hahm*) for the bride. Usually, the gifts are jewelry and red and blue fabric for a traditional dress. Friends of the groom **deliver** the box at night. They **shout** playfully, "Buy a hahm! Hahm for sale!" The friends wait for the family to give them food and money, then they give the box of gifts to the girl.

6 The day of the wedding arrives! Traditionally, the groom first gives his new mother-**in-law** the gift of a goose. The goose is a symbol of love because a goose takes only one partner in its life. Today, the groom gives

(continued)

a goose made of wood. Then it's time for the ceremony. They have the ceremony at a table. The bride and groom sit at the table. They each have a cup full of a special wine, and they **take a sip**. Then someone takes the cups, mixes together the wine, and pours it into their cups again. The bride and groom each sip the mixed wine. This is a symbol of their new life together.

7 Korean Americans have a ceremony that is a little different. Family and close friends attend the ceremony. The new wife offers her in-laws gifts of dried fruits that represent children. This is a symbol of her wish to give them grandchildren. Her in-laws offer her tea. At the end of the ceremony, they throw fruit and chestnuts at the bride, and she tries to catch them in her skirt.

8 The wedding **banquet** follows. It is called "the noodle banquet" because there is a lot of noodle soup. As in China, noodles represent a long and happy life. For dessert, there are sweet cakes and a sweet, sticky rice ball. It has chestnuts, jujubes, raisins, and pine nuts. These are all symbols of children.

9 When the eldest son of a family gets married, it is traditional for his parents to move in with him and his new wife. This shows that the son will always take care of his parents, and that his wife will take care of his parents also.

VOCABULARY

MEANING

Write the correct words in the blanks.

match	deliver	ceremony	exchange
banquet	document	hired	shout

1. In the past, parents paid a woman to find a bride or groom for their children. They _____ her.

2. The woman tried to find a good _____ for their son or daughter. She looked for two people who were like each other.

3. For the engagement, the families get together and do and say special things. They have a _____.

4. The girl gives the boy a gift, and the boy gives the girl a gift. They
   _____ gifts.
5. The boy gives the girl a special piece of paper, or a _____.
6. Friends of the groom go to the girl's house and give her a box. They
   _____ the box to the house.
7. The friends are not quiet. They _____ "Buy a hahm!"
8. There is a special dinner with many people, or a _____, after
   the wedding ceremony.

WORDS THAT GO TOGETHER

Write the correct words in the blanks.

get engaged	set a date	in-law	take a sip

1. After the bride and groom get married, the groom is related to the bride's
   mother. She is his mother- _____.
2. The two families decide on a day to have the wedding. They
   _____ _____ for the wedding.
3. Many couples don't get married immediately. They
   _____ _____, then wait a while to get married.
4. The bride and the groom drink some of the special wine. They

   _____.

USE

Work with a partner to answer the questions. Use complete sentences.

1. What famous couple do you think is a good *match*?
2. Do you have a traditional or modern wedding *ceremony* in your country,
   or both?
3. At what time do people usually *exchange* gifts?
4. What is an important *document* that you have?
5. What is something that people *deliver*?
6. When do you usually *shout*?
7. When do people usually have a *banquet*?

COMPREHENSION

UNDERSTANDING THE READING

Circle the letter of the correct answer.

1. Before Koreans get married, they _____.
   a. go to a fortune-teller
   b. have a banquet
   c. meet at the boy's house
   d. throw fruit

2. At the engagement ceremony, _____.
   a. the girl's family gives gifts only
   b. the two families meet with the fortune-teller
   c. the two families give each other documents
   d. the two families meet and give gifts

3. At the wedding ceremony, _____.
   a. the bride gets a goose
   b. the mother-in-law gives a goose
   c. the bride and groom sit at a table
   d. the bride gets a box of gifts

REMEMBERING DETAILS

Reread the passage and answer the questions.

1. What are the four pillars?
2. Who predicts the boy's and girl's destiny?
3. What does the girl keep all her life?
4. When do the friends of the groom deliver the box?
5. Why is the goose a symbol of love?
6. What do noodles represent?

MAKING INFERENCES

All of the statements below are true. Some of them are stated directly in the reading. Others can be inferred, or guessed, from the reading. Write *S* for each stated fact. Write *I* for each inference.

_____ 1. The couple can get engaged if the fortune-teller says their four pillars are good.

_____ 2. If the four pillars are not good, the matchmaker has to find another partner.

_____ 3. Parents play an important part when a couple gets married.

_____ 4. It is a custom for the eldest son and his new bride to live with his mother and father.

_____ 5. Today, many Koreans live in cities; in the past, more families lived on farms.

TELL THE STORY

Work with a partner or together as a class. Tell the story of how Koreans celebrate a wedding. Use your own words. Your partner or other students can ask questions about the story.

DISCUSSION

Discuss the answers to these questions with your classmates.

1. Do you think arranged marriages are a good or bad idea? Give reasons.
2. Do you think it is a good idea to see a fortune-teller before a marriage or other important event?
3. Who pays for a wedding and/or an engagement ceremony in your country?

WRITING

Write six sentences or a short paragraph about a wedding or similar ceremony in your country.

Example: *My sister had a wedding ceremony in church. She wore a beautiful white dress.*

_____

_____

_____

_____

_____

_____

SPELLING AND PUNCTUATION

COLONS

> **We use a colon (:) to introduce a list of items at the end of a sentence or to give an explanation.**
>
> List of items   *Koreans believe in the "four pillars":* **the year, month, day, and hour of a person's birth.**
>
> Explanation   *The first is by love match:* **two people meet, fall in love, and get married.**
>
> **We do <u>not</u> use a colon after the words** *such as, especially, like,* **and** *including.*

Put colons in the correct places. Some sentences do not need a colon.

1. They give gifts such as jewelry, red fabric, and blue fabric.
2. The sweet rice ball has the following raisins, chestnuts, pine nuts, and jujubes.
3. In Korea, there are three kinds of wedding ceremonies Eastern, Western, and a mix of the two.
4. Korea has two parts North Korea and South Korea.
5. An engagement ceremony can take place in any of these places the girl's house, a hotel, or a restaurant.
6. On the wedding table there are many things including two candlesticks, chestnuts, and branches of special trees.
7. The second way is an arranged marriage a third person chooses two people to marry each other, and if the two families agree, the next step is to visit the fortune-teller.
8. They hire a matchmaker a woman who they pay to find a good husband or wife for their daughter or son.
9. The groom's family sends a *hahm* a box of gifts for the bride.
10. The groom gives his mother-in-law a gift of a goose a symbol of love because the goose takes only one partner in its life.

UNIT 12

Why Are Sumo Wrestlers So Fat?

BEFORE YOU READ

Answer these questions.

1. What do you know about wrestling?
2. What is special about sumo wrestling?
3. Why is sumo wrestling popular?

Why Are Sumo Wrestlers So Fat?

1 It is very difficult to stop a train, a ship, or any large object that is moving. The same is true for a sumo wrestler. A big wrestler is hard to move. It is easier for him to move you—like a train that hits a bicycle.

2 Sumo is a kind of wrestling that comes from Japan. It is Japan's national sport. The **origin** of sumo wrestling is religious. It came from Japan's Shinto religion. You can see the effect of the religion in every part of the sport. For example, the ring, or *dohyo*, looks like a Shinto temple. The *dohyo* is fifteen feet across and two feet high. All the decorations are Shinto symbols, too.

3 Each sumo match starts with a traditional ceremony. The ceremony is as important as the wrestling, and the people like to watch it. Each movement in the ceremony has a special meaning. To begin the ceremony, the wrestlers face each other and **raise** their arms. In the past, this was to show that they didn't have any knives. Then they **clap their hands** and **stamp their feet**. In the past, this was to **chase away** demons, or bad spirits. Each wrestler has a unique style for his movements. One wrestler may finish the ceremony in one minute, another may take three minutes. The last part of the ceremony is to throw salt in the ring. This means that the ring is clean and ready to use.

4 After the ceremony, the wrestling match starts. The **basic** rules of sumo are simple and few, which means that matches can be very exciting. During the match the wrestler can't pull hair, hit with a closed **fist**, or choke the other wrestler (but he may push at his throat). He can do anything else. The first wrestler who touches the ground with anything except his feet or steps out of the ring is the loser. Five judges watch the match. A match only lasts a few seconds and rarely lasts one minute.

5 To become a sumo wrestler you must first join a stable. To enter a stable, you must be fifteen to twenty-two years old. You must be at least five feet seven inches tall and weigh at least 165 pounds. Parents must agree to let their son join a stable, and he must pass a physical exam. When he joins a stable, a wrestler trains and lives there. He is part of that stable for the rest of his life.

6 In a stable, **rank** is extremely important. New members start training at 4:30 or 5:00 A.M. In the beginning, new wrestlers do the housework nobody likes. They prepare lunch, clean, wash clothes, and do many other chores. Wrestlers of low rank always **serve** wrestlers of high rank.

7 Weight is important to sumo wrestlers. When they join a stable, wrestlers may weigh less than 200 pounds, but they must **gain weight** to advance. The average weight of a top-rank wrestler is 335 pounds. Wrestlers are big, but they are not all fat. They have strong muscles in their arms and legs. They are also very **flexible**. Some sumo wrestlers have less body fat than the average businessman. Weight is important, but they must also have speed, strength, balance, and technique. Sumo wrestlers can have health problems because of their weight, too. They often have heart trouble, high blood pressure, diabetes, and injuries from wrestling. Most wrestlers try to lose weight after they **retire**.

8 It is not easy for some wrestlers to get big. They don't eat candy or other junk food to gain weight. They eat large portions of high-calorie food with lots of rice. Some wrestlers eat 20,000 calories a day. That's ten times the calories an **average** person eats. They also exercise a lot to build muscle.

9 In Japan, sumo wrestlers are national heroes. They are as popular as movie stars. The Japanese believe that sumo wrestlers bring good luck. If a sumo wrestler of high rank picks up a baby, the baby will grow big and strong. They are also popular with women. Sumo wrestlers often marry models, actresses, or television stars.

VOCABULARY

MEANING

Write the correct words in the blanks.

retire	average	basic	fist	serve
ranks	flexible	origin	raise	

1. The beginning, or _____, of sumo is religious.
2. First, the wrestlers _____ their arms. They lift their arms up high.
3. The main, or _____, rules of sumo are simple.
4. A wrestler cannot hit the other wrestler with his hands and fingers closed. He can't hit with his _____.
5. Sumo wrestlers in a stable have different levels, or _____.
6. A new wrestler in a stable must _____ an older wrestler. He must do things for and bring food and drinks to the older wrestler.
7. Wrestlers are big, but they can bend into every position very quickly and easily. They are _____.
8. When sumo wrestlers stop work, they _____.
9. A sumo wrestler eats much more than other people. He eats ten times as much as the _____ man.

WORDS THAT GO TOGETHER

Write the correct words in the blanks.

stamp their feet	chase away	gain weight	clap their hands

1. The wrestlers make noise by hitting their hands together over and over. They _____.
2. The wrestlers also _____. They lift their feet and put them down hard.
3. With all this noise they _____ the bad spirits. They make the spirits leave.
4. Sumo wrestlers have to be very heavy. If a wrestler isn't heavy, he must _____.

Work with a partner to answer the questions. Use complete sentences.

1. What is the *origin* of your name?
2. When do you *raise* your arm in class?
3. What is a *basic* spelling or punctuation rule in English?
4. At what age do people in your country usually *retire*?
5. What is something that is *flexible*?
6. What is the *average* age of the students in your class?
7. When do you usually *clap your hands*?

COMPREHENSION

UNDERSTANDING THE READING

Circle the letter of the correct answer.

1. Sumo is _____.
   a. Japan's national sport
   b. a Japanese religion
   c. a traditional kind of ceremony
   d. a symbol of Shinto

2. A sumo match starts with a _____.
   a. long ceremony
   b. traditional ceremony
   c. special meaning
   d. national ceremony

3. Sumo wrestlers must _____.
   a. not gain weight in a stable
   b. be popular to advance
   c. gain weight to advance
   d. be good businessmen to advance

REMEMBERING DETAILS

Reread the passage and answer the questions.

1. What does a sumo ring look like?
2. What do the wrestlers do to begin the ceremony?
3. What do they do at the end of the ceremony?
4. How many judges are there?
5. How much must a man weigh to join a stable?
6. How long does a match usually last?

MAKING INFERENCES

All of the statements below are true. Some of them are stated directly in the reading. Others can be inferred, or guessed, from the reading. Write *S* for each stated fact. Write *I* for each inference.

_____ 1. To become a sumo wrestler you must learn to control yourself and obey.

_____ 2. Sumo wrestlers are big, but they are not slow.

_____ 3. Sumo wrestlers often die young.

_____ 4. New wrestlers do a lot of chores in a stable.

_____ 5. A wrestler cannot change his stable after he joins.

TELL THE STORY

Work with a partner or together as a class. Tell the story of sumo wrestlers. Use your own words. Your partner or other students can ask questions about the story.

DISCUSSION

Discuss the answers to these questions with your classmates.

1. Who are some popular sports stars around the world? Why are they popular?

2. Do you think sports stars should make a lot of money like movie stars?

3. Do you want to be a famous sports star? Why or why not?

WRITING

Write six sentences or a short paragraph about your favorite sports or movie star.

Example: *My favorite sports star is Tiger Woods. I like him because he is a nice person, and he works very hard.*

_____

_____

_____

_____

_____

_____

SPELLING AND PUNCTUATION

MEASUREMENT WORDS

We use measurement words every day at school, work, and home.

The average weight of a top-rank wrestler is 335 **pounds.**

You must be at least five **feet** *seven* **inches** *tall.*

Here are some U.S. measurement words and their abbreviations. In longer pieces of writing, we usually spell out the measurements. In shorter writing, as well as charts, graphs, and forms, we often abbreviate.

Remember that people in the United States do not usually use the metric system. Sometimes people use it for medical, military, or scientific material.

Units	Abbreviation	Metric Units	Abbreviation
inch	*in. or "*	*meter*	*m.*
foot	*ft. or '*	*kilometer*	*km.*
pint	*pt.*	*liter*	*l.*
gallon	*gal.*		
ounce	*oz.*	*gram*	*g.*
pound	*lb.*	*kilogram*	*kg.*
ton	*tn.*	*tonne*	*t.*

Here are the words and abbreviations for time measurement.

hour	*hr.*	*minute*	*min.*	*second*	*sec.*

For sentences with abbreviations, write out the measurement words on the lines. For sentences with measurement words, write the abbreviations on the lines.

1. The *dohyo* is fifteen feet across and two feet high. _____

2. He is at least 180 lbs. _____

3. The match lasted one minute and two seconds. _____

4. He performed the ceremony in one min. and thirty secs. _____

5. The wrestlers eat three lbs. of rice every day. _____

6. He drinks one gal. of water every day. _____

7. He practices for three hrs. in the morning. _____

8. This dish has twelve ounces of fat. _____

9. He is so strong that he can lift one tn. _____

10. His chest measures sixty in. across. _____

UNIT 13

Who Is Stephen King?

BEFORE YOU READ

Answer these questions.

1. Do you like horror movies? Why or why not?
2. What makes you very scared in a movie?
3. What is a famous horror story or book you know?

Who Is Stephen King?

1 Stephen King is one of the world's most famous writers. He has sold more books than any other American writer. His most popular works are horror, or **scary**, stories. But it isn't only his books that are popular. People all over the world **line up** to see the movies made from his books, movies like *Carrie*, *The Shining*, and *The Dead Zone*.

2 Stephen King was born in 1947 in Portland, Maine. When he was two, his father **abandoned** the family. His mother had to take care of Stephen and his older brother alone. They moved **from place to place** because it was hard for his mother to find work. It was a difficult time, and they had little money. In the evenings, Stephen's mother read to him. His favorite story was *The Strange Case of Dr. Jekyl and Mr. Hyde*. Later, Stephen read the book himself. He wanted to write a story like it, but he wanted his story to be scarier. Stephen started to write his own stories when he was about seven. His mother always **encouraged** him and sent his stories to publishers. By age eighteen, Stephen published his first story.

3 Stephen graduated from high school in 1966 and **went straight** to college. He studied very hard and always worked in his free time to make extra money. King graduated in 1970. He wanted to be a teacher, but he couldn't find work right away. He had to work at a gas station, then at a laundry service. King finally got a job teaching English at a private high school in Maine. That year Stephen married Tabitha Spruce, his college girlfriend. Tabitha was also a writer. They were happy, but they didn't have much money. They didn't even have a telephone!

4 King wrote a novel titled *Carrie*, but he thought no one would like it. This made him sad and angry, so he **threw** the book **away**. Tabitha saw him throw away all the pages and was also angry. She took the pages from the **trash**. She liked the story very much and thought other people would like it, too. She **persuaded** him to send his book to a publisher. Later, King got a telegram from the publisher. He read it and was shocked. They wanted to publish *Carrie*!

5 At first, bookstores sold only 13,000 copies of the book. Stephen and Tabitha were happy with that, but other people had bigger ideas. A company wanted to make a movie from the book, and Stephen agreed.

(continued)

After the movie, the book sold 3.5 million copies. The publisher told King he would **earn** $400,000. King couldn't believe it.

6 King immediately wanted to buy his wife a **fancy** present. He went to many stores on the way home, but everything was closed except the drugstore. He went in and looked for something nice to give Tabitha, but the drugstore didn't have fancy gifts. He wanted to bring her something, so he bought her a hair dryer.

7 Now that they had money from the book, Stephen and Tabitha didn't have to keep their jobs. They were both going to be full-time writers. Stephen King soon published more books and became rich and famous. He bought a big house in Maine for his wife and three children. It was a house that his wife always liked, but they couldn't afford it before his books became popular. It's an old house with twenty-three bedrooms. Today they live in the same house, and Stephen still works extremely hard. He works every day of the year except three: Christmas, the Fourth of July, and his birthday. He always writes six pages a day, and he usually works on two different books at the same time.

8 In June of 1999, King was in a bad accident. As he was walking along the road near his house, a van hit him. King had to have three operations on his legs and hips. People thought he might have to stop writing. It took a long time, but King **recovered** and continued with his work **as usual**. Does he ever think he will stop writing? He says he will stop when he can't find more stories—but Stephen King always finds more stories.

VOCABULARY

MEANING

Write the correct words in the blanks.

fancy	trash	encouraged	abandoned
earn	persuaded	scary	recovered

1. Stephen King writes stories that make people afraid. They are _____ stories.

2. Stephen's father _____ his wife and children. He left and never came back again.

3. Stephen's mother supported him and told him he was a great writer. She _____ him to keep writing.

4. Stephen did not want the book anymore, so he threw out the book in the _____.

5. Tabitha talked to Stephen and changed his mind. She _____ him to send the book to a publisher.

6. King couldn't believe he would _____ so much money from his book.

7. At first, Stephen bought a simple gift for his wife. Then he paid more money and bought a _____ gift for her.

8. King was very sick after the accident, but after a long time he _____ and was well again.

WORDS THAT GO TOGETHER

Write the correct words in the blanks.

threw away	went straight	line up	from place to place	as usual

1. When there is a good movie, people _____ in front of the theater to see it.

2. Stephen, his brother, and his mother did not stay in one town. They moved _____.

3. After high school, King _____ to college. He didn't do anything in between.

4. King continued to do his work the same way he always did. He did his work _____.

5. King did not want to see his book, so he _____ the book in the trash.

Work with a partner to answer the questions. Use complete sentences.

1. What is the name of a *scary* movie or book you know?
2. When do you go to a *fancy* restaurant?
3. How long does it take to *recover* from a cold?
4. How much does a doctor *earn* in your country?
5. Who *encourages* you to learn English?
6. Where do you usually *line up*?
7. Where do you *go straight* after class?

COMPREHENSION

UNDERSTANDING THE READING

Circle the letter of the correct answer.

1. Stephen King is famous for _____.
    a. writing *The Strange Case of Dr. Jekyl and Mr. Hyde*
    b. writing scary books and movies
    c. publishing a story when he was seven years old
    d. selling more books than any writer in the world

2. After the movie *Carrie*, Stephen King _____.
    a. sold a lot of books
    b. wrote the book *Carrie*
    c. married Tabitha
    d. threw away the book

3. After the accident, Stephen King _____.
    a. moved from his house
    b. stopped writing
    c. continued writing
    d. recovered quickly

REMEMBERING DETAILS

Reread the passage and fill in the blanks.

1. After King graduated in 1970, he worked at a _____, then at a _____.

2. His college girlfriend Tabitha was a _____.

3. After the movie *Carrie*, the book sold _____ copies.

4. He wanted to buy his wife a gift, so he went to the drugstore and bought her a _____.

5. King works every day except: _____, _____, and _____.

6. After the accident, King had to have _____ on his legs and hips.

MAKING INFERENCES

All of the statements below are true. Some of them are stated directly in the reading. Others can be inferred, or guessed, from the reading. Write S for each stated fact. Write I for each inference.

____ 1. Money and fame have not changed Stephen King.

____ 2. King started to write as a young boy and continues to this day.

____ 3. Stephen and Tabitha have a happy marriage.

____ 4. Stephen King has liked scary stories since he was a child.

____ 5. It is easy for King to find stories to write about.

TELL THE STORY

Work with a partner or together as a class. Tell the story of Stephen King. Use your own words. Your partner or other students can ask questions about the story.

DISCUSSION

Discuss the answers to these questions with your classmates.

1. Why do some people like horror stories?

2. Do you prefer to see a movie or read a book about the same subject?

3. Stephen King is now rich and famous, but he has not changed. Why do some people change when they become rich and famous?

WRITING

Write six sentences or a short paragraph about a movie you liked.

Example: *Last week, I saw a movie about a man who had a special power. He could see things in the future.*

_____

_____

_____

_____

_____

_____

SPELLING AND PUNCTUATION

TITLES OF WORKS: ITALICS AND UNDERLINING

> **Titles of works such as movies, books, magazines, plays, and television programs need special treatment. When we use a computer, we use *italics*. When we write by hand or use a typewriter, we <u>underline</u>.**
>
> Movies like *The Shining* and *The Dead Zone* were made from Stephen King's books. (computer)
>
> Movies like <u>The Shining</u> and <u>The Dead Zone</u> were made from Stephen King's books. (handwriting and typing)
>
> His favorite book was *The Strange Case of Dr. Jekyl and Mr. Hyde*. (computer)
>
> His favorite book was <u>The Strange Case of Dr. Jekyl and Mr. Hyde</u>. (handwriting and typing)

Underline the titles of works.

1. Have you seen the movie The Silence of the Lambs?
2. King wrote about movies in the book The Horror Writer and the Ten Bears.
3. King's first story was published in Comics Review.
4. King's The Talisman has a similar story to The Lord of the Rings.
5. Mary Wollstonecraft Shelley's Frankenstein is a popular horror story.
6. King has had five of his books on The New York Times bestseller list at the same time.
7. I saw the movie Carrie with Sissy Spacek.
8. King wrote a TV series called The Golden Years.

UNIT 14

What Is the Story Behind the Bed?

BEFORE YOU READ

Answer these questions.

1. What kind of bed do you like to sleep in?
2. What kinds of beds are there?
3. How do you think people slept a few hundred years ago?

What Is the Story Behind the Bed?

1 People spend about one-third of their lives asleep. We can survive longer without food than without sleep. Sleeping is very important, so the bed is important. Scientists say that the first bed was probably some leaves. Now, of course, beds are much better than that, and we have lots of **choices**. An average bed today lasts about fifteen years, and most people change beds about five times in their life. Even with all the beds in the world, people still invent new ones. And some people are still searching for the perfect bed.

2 For most of human history, people slept on layers of cloth, palm leaves, or furs. They laid these on the floor. In ancient Egypt, over three thousand years ago, the pharaohs were the first to raise their beds off the floor. They slept on light beds made of wood. You could **fold** the bed and carry it. Archaeologists found beds like this in Tutankhamen's tomb. People back then did not think soft pillows were **necessary**. The Egyptians put their heads on headrests made of wood and the Chinese had ceramic headrests.

3 After the year 100, only the rich had beds. Poor people still slept on the floor. The bed became a symbol of **wealth**. One emperor of Rome had a silver bed. Beds were also a person's most valuable **possession**. When Shakespeare died, he gave his second best bed to his wife. Beds were so special that in England, when a rich person traveled to another person's home, he took his bed with him. When a person stayed at a hotel for the night, he had to share a bed with strangers. If a rich person came to the hotel, the manager threw a poor traveler out of a bed to make room. All this sharing meant that beds were not very clean, and insects lived in them. Some people, **especially** rich women, slept on a chair when they traveled.

4 After 1750, beds became beautiful pieces of furniture. They were made of carved wood. A beautiful bed at that time could cost $1 million in today's money. The beds had four posts, one on each corner. People used these to hang curtains around the bed. The curtains helped to keep the bed warm. Also, because you passed through one room to get to another, the curtains were good for **privacy**.

5 Beds also became higher and higher. Queen Victoria slept on a bed with seven mattresses on top of each other. She had steps beside the bed to reach the top. Mattresses usually had straw on the inside (for poor people) or feathers (for the rich). After 1820, people slept on cotton mattresses with metal springs inside them. Beds made of metal became popular, too. The best beds were made of a yellow metal called brass. Metal beds were better for your health than beds made of wood, because they had fewer insects in them. That's why hospital beds are metal today.

6 In ancient Rome, people slept in their everyday clothes. In England, people did not wear clothes in bed. They wore a cap to keep their head and ears warm. Later, men wore nightshirts and women wore long nightdresses and hats. **It was only after** 1890 that men started to wear pajamas.

7 People had interesting ways to **keep warm** in bed. Many families shared one big bed. Some people had a small dog in bed to keep their feet warm. Sometimes, people warmed the bed before they got into it. They warmed stones, wrapped them in cloth, and put them in the bed. Later, they used bottles with hot water inside. One English Prime Minister, William Gladstone, filled his bottle with tea **in case** he was thirsty at night.

8 Some people in Asian cultures prefer to sleep on the floor. They sleep on a thick mattress of cloth layers called a futon. They can roll up the futon and put it away during the day. Some people put their futon on a low frame rather than on the floor. Then it looks a lot like a Western-style bed.

9 Beds today come in every size and shape. We have round beds, king-size beds, bunk beds, **adjustable** beds, waterbeds, airbeds, and futons. Are you feeling sleepy yet? Sweet dreams!

VOCABULARY

MEANING

Write the correct words in the blanks.

wealth	necessary	choices	possession
especially	privacy	fold	adjustable

1. Today, there are many kinds of beds. We have many _____.
2. In the past, people thought it was not important or _____ to have soft pillows under your head.

3. The pharaohs in Egypt had beds you could bend back, or _____. Then the pharaohs could carry them.

4. Rich people had expensive beds to show their _____.

5. The bed was a valuable _____, or something valuable you owned.

6. Rich people did not like to sleep in dirty beds, _____ rich women.

7. There are beds today that you can move to any position. They are _____.

8. People who did not want others to see them put curtains around their bed for _____

WORDS THAT GO TOGETHER

Write the correct words in the blanks.

it was only after	keep warm	in case

1. People do not want to be cold in bed. They want to _____.

2. Long ago, mattresses were made of straw. _____ 1820 that people used cotton mattresses.

3. Sometimes William Gladstone was thirsty at night, and sometimes he wasn't. He kept tea in his bed _____ he wanted a drink.

USE

Work with a partner to answer the questions. Use complete sentences.

1. What is something in your house that you *fold*?
2. What shows *wealth* today?
3. What is something *necessary* to have in your English class?
4. What is your most valuable *possession*?
5. What do people do for *privacy* in their bedroom?
6. What do you put on a bed to *keep warm*?
7. What do you keep in your house *in case* the electricity goes out?

COMPREHENSION

Circle the letter of the correct answer.

1. After the year 100, the bed was _____.
   a. made of leaves
   b. not important
   c. a symbol of wealth
   d. only in hotels

2. Beds made of metal were _____.
   a. higher
   b. better for your health
   c. more expensive
   d. like beautiful pieces of furniture

3. To keep warm, people _____.
   a. put warm stones in the bed
   b. wrapped their feet in cloth
   c. drank tea in bed
   d. warmed themselves before they got in the bed

REMEMBERING DETAILS

Reread the passage and answer the questions.

1. What kind of headrests did the Egyptians have?
2. To whom did Shakespeare give his second best bed?
3. What did people hang around the bed?
4. Why did they do this?
5. How many mattresses did Queen Victoria have on her bed?
6. Why were metal beds better for your health?
7. What do people in some Asian cultures sleep on?

All of the statements below are true. Some of them are stated directly in the reading. Others can be inferred, or guessed, from the reading. Write *S* for each stated fact. Write *I* for each inference.

_____ 1.   Sleep is more important than food.

_____ 2.   Manufacturers today don't make beds that last a lifetime because they want to sell more beds.

_____ 3.   Beds were not clean in the past.

_____ 4.   Asian cultures use a futon because they don't have space for a permanent bed.

_____ 5.   In the past, people covered their heads to keep warm in bed.

TELL THE STORY

Work with a partner or together as a class. Tell the story of the bed. Use your own words. Your partner or other students can ask questions about the story.

DISCUSSION

Discuss the answers to these questions with your classmates.

1.   What kinds of clothes do people sleep in?
2.   Do you think where you sleep affects how well you sleep?
3.   What do you know about beds in different countries? For example, some people use pillow-top mattresses, Americans have "king-size" beds, the French use a traversin—a long sausage-type pillow. What do the different beds say about the people?

WRITING

Write six sentences or a short paragraph about your bed and how you sleep.

Example: *I sleep on a bed with a soft mattress. My bed is new and was very expensive. I use three pillows under my head.*

_____

_____

_____

_____

_____

_____

SPELLING AND PUNCTUATION

COMMAS: AFTER PREPOSITIONAL PHRASES

There are different phrases to begin sentences. One type of phrase is a prepositional phrase. We use a comma after a prepositional phrase at the beginning of a sentence. A prepositional phrase begins with a preposition (*after, in, on, by, at, for, with, without*). Remember that a phrase does not have a subject and a verb.

In ancient Egypt, pharaohs slept on beds.

After the year 100, only the rich had beds.

After a while, they used bottles with hot water inside.

A. Rewrite the sentences with commas in the correct places.

1. After 1750 beds became beautiful.

   _____

2. In England people started to put curtains around the bed.

   _____

3. In fact the kind of curtain you had around the bed showed your wealth.

   _____

4. In the winter people warmed their beds.

   _____

5. On hot nights there were many insects in the bedroom.

   _____

6. By 1900 men started to wear pajamas to bed.

   _____

7. At this time the brass bed became popular.

   _____

8. With brass beds bedrooms had fewer insects.

   _____

9. In Japan people sleep on a futon that they roll up during the day.

   _____

10. At this time there are beds of every size and shape.

    _____

UNIT 15

How Did the Spanish Conquer the Aztecs?

BEFORE YOU READ

Answer these questions.

1. Who were the Aztecs and where did they live?
2. What do you know about the Aztecs' lives?
3. Where are the descendants of the Aztecs today?

How Did the Spanish Conquer the Aztecs?

1 Hundreds of years ago, there was a beautiful city on an island in the middle of a lake. It had buildings, roads, and palaces. In many ways, it was like London, which was the biggest city in the world at the time. But this city was thousands of miles away from London. It was the **capital** of the Aztec empire, an empire that controlled about six million people. It was the seat of government, the religious center, and the cultural center of Aztec life. This beautiful city was Tenochtitlán. Today we call it Mexico City.

2 Hernán Cortés was a Spanish explorer. He left Spain when he was only nineteen to explore and settle the island of Cuba. But Cortés didn't want to live in Cuba. He wanted to explore and to be rich and famous. The Spanish government told him to explore what is today Mexico. Cortés was excited. He knew stories about the Aztecs. He heard the Aztecs had gold. In 1519, he and about 400 men sailed from Cuba to the coast of what is today Mexico. They were afraid. They heard stories that the Aztecs **sacrificed** people to their gods. And the Aztecs had an army of more than one million men. Cortés thought they didn't **have a chance**, but they got lucky—very lucky.

3 The Aztecs believed in many gods. One of the most **terrible** gods was Tezcatlipoca, or the Smoking Mirror. This god **watched over** the land and made the Aztecs powerful. Another of their gods was Quetzalcoatl, or the Feathered Serpent. They believed he lived in a strange land in the east across the sea. This god once came to earth as a white man with a black beard. He brought knowledge to the people, and the Aztecs liked him. This made the Smoking Mirror angry, so he forced the Feathered Serpent to go away. The Feathered Serpent promised to come back one day and become the ruler of the Aztecs. The Aztec priests predicted that the Feathered Serpent would come back during a special year on their calendar. That year was 1519.

4 In 1519, many **strange** things happened, like earthquakes. There was also a comet, which is a bright object that moves around the sun. People were waiting to see what would happen next. The emperor of the Aztecs was worried. He thought the Feathered Serpent would come and he would not be emperor anymore. Then his men saw Cortés. He had white

(*continued*)

skin and a black beard, just like the Feathered Serpent, and he came from the east in the Feathered Serpent's special year. The biggest **coincidence** was that Cortés came to the Aztec empire on April 21. This was the day **dedicated to** the Feathered Serpent. This persuaded the Aztec emperor that Cortés was the Feathered Serpent. He sent his men to greet him and welcomed him to the city. He gave Cortés gifts of gold and jewels and gave him and his men a palace for their home.

5 Cortés and his men could not believe their luck. They didn't know about the many coincidences working **in their favor**. They took everything the Aztecs gave them. Soon they became arrogant and decided to take the city and the empire for Spain. They made the emperor their prisoner. **Meanwhile**, one of Cortés's men killed a group of Aztecs at a religious ceremony. All of this made the Aztecs very angry. Cortés tried to **calm** them **down**. He showed them their emperor, but this didn't help. The emperor got hurt and later died. Nobody knows who killed him. Then the Aztecs threw Cortés and his men out of the capital.

6 Cortés still wanted to **conquer** the city, so he came back two years later with his men. It was his second trip there. They and many natives who didn't like the Aztec government destroyed the palace and other buildings and killed many people. They took over the city and settled there. Cortés made the Aztec empire a **colony** of Spain. In 1820, that same land, Mexico, became an **independent** country.

7 Today, Mexico City is one of the biggest cities in the world. Many Mexicans are descendants of the Aztecs. More than one million Mexicans speak the Aztec native language, Nahuatl, as their first language. The old buildings and statues of the Aztecs **mix** with the modern buildings of Mexico City so that everyone remembers the city's rich history.

VOCABULARY

MEANING

Write the correct words in the blanks.

colony	strange	sacrificed	terrible	coincidence
conquer	mix	meanwhile	capital	independent

1. Mexico's central government is in Mexico City. It is the _____ of Mexico today.

2. The Aztecs killed people and animals and _____ them. They offered the people and animals to their gods in ceremonies.

3. One god was very, very bad. He was a _____ god.

4. Many _____ things happened in 1519. People did not understand the unusual events.

5. Cortés came to the Aztec empire on the same day that was dedicated to the Feathered Serpent god. This was a _____.

6. The Aztec emperor was a prisoner of Cortés. _____, or, during this time, one of Cortés's men killed some Aztecs.

7. Spain controlled the Aztec empire. The empire was a _____ of Spain.

8. In 1820, Mexico became a free or _____ country.

9. There are many different buildings and structures in Mexico City. It is a _____ of modern and ancient.

10. Cortés wanted to fight and win control of the Aztecs. He wanted to _____ them.

WORDS THAT GO TOGETHER

Write the correct words in the blanks.

calm down	dedicated to	have a chance
watched over	in their favor	

1. Cortés and his 400 men could not fight against one million men. He didn't _____.

2. The Smoking Mirror god _____ the land of the Aztecs and protected it.

3. April 21 was a special day for the Feathered Serpent god. It was a day _____ him.

4. The Aztecs were angry. Cortés tried to _____ the Aztecs so they would not be so angry.

5. Cortés and his men were very lucky. Everything that happened helped them. Things were _____.

USE

Work with a partner to answer the questions. Use complete sentences.

1. What is the *capital* city of your country?
2. What country was a *colony* of another country in the past?
3. What do you do to *calm down* when you are upset?
4. Who *watched over* you when you were a child?
5. When did your country become *independent*?
6. What colors can you *mix* to get another color?

COMPREHENSION

UNDERSTANDING THE READING

Circle the letter of the correct answer.

1. Hernán Cortés wanted to _____.
   a. live in Cuba
   b. get the gold of the Aztecs
   c. get money from Spain
   d. be an Aztec emporer

2. At first, the Aztecs _____.
   a. did not like Cortés
   b. attacked Cortés
   c. thought Cortés was one of their gods
   d. thought Cortés was a priest

3. Today, the Aztecs _____.
   a. have descendants in Mexico
   b. have nothing to show their history
   c. have become Spanish
   d. all live in Mexico City

REMEMBERING DETAILS

Reread the passage and answer the questions.

1. Where did Cortés go after he left Spain?
2. Why were Cortés and his men afraid?
3. What did the Feathered Serpent god look like?
4. What did the Aztec emperor give Cortés and his men?
5. When did Mexico become an independent country?
6. How many Mexicans speak the native language of the Aztecs?

MAKING INFERENCES

All of the statements below are true. Some of then are stated directly in the reading. Others can be inferred, or guessed, from the reading. Write *S* for each stated fact. Write *I* for each inference.

_____ 1. Cortés's men were afraid to go to Mexico.

_____ 2. The Aztecs had an advanced civilization

_____ 3. The Aztecs believed in good and bad gods.

_____ 4. Cortés and his men were lucky the Aztecs did not attack them.

_____ 5. The Aztec emperor suffered a lot from the Spanish.

TELL THE STORY

Work with a partner or together as a class. Tell the story of how the Spanish conquered Mexico City. Use your own words. Your partner or other students can ask questions about the story.

DISCUSSION

Discuss the answers to these questions with your classmates.

1. Do you believe in luck? If so, talk about a time when you had good luck or bad luck. If not, discuss why you don't believe in it.
2. Have you experienced a coincidence? Discuss.
3. Mexico City is a combination of old and new buildings. What type of building do you prefer? Do you think it is a good idea to mix different types of buildings in one area? Give examples and explain.

WRITING

Write six sentences or a short paragraph about a lucky day or a coincidence.

Example: *I had a strange coincidence about a year ago. One morning I was in line to enroll for my classes . . .*

_____

_____

_____

_____

_____

_____

SPELLING AND PUNCTUATION

CARDINAL NUMBERS AND ORDINAL NUMBERS

Cardinal numbers are the regular numbers we use to show quantity.

*In 1519, he and about **400** men sailed from Cuba to the coast of what is today Mexico.*

We use ordinal numbers when we want to show where something comes in a series.

*It was his **second** trip.*

To write ordinal numbers, we put the two last letters of the ordinal number after the number in figures. For example, we can write *first* as *1st*, *thirty-second* as *32nd*, and *fifteenth* as *15th*.

1st	first	9th	ninth	17th	seventeenth
2nd	second	10th	tenth	18th	eighteenth
3rd	third	11th	eleventh	19th	nineteenth
4th	fourth	12th	twelfth	20th	twentieth
5th	fifth	13th	thirteenth	21st	twenty-first
6th	sixth	14th	fourteenth	100th	one hundreth
7th	seventh	15th	fifteenth	1000th	one thousandth
8th	eighth	16th	sixteenth	1,000,000th	one millionth

A. Rewrite the sentences using ordinal numbers.

1. Cortés went to Cuba on his 1 voyage.

   _____

2. The Aztec emperor died on the 3 day after he was made a prisoner.

   _____

3. My parents went to Mexico for their 20 wedding anniversary.

   _____

4. Today, Mexico City is the 12 most populated city in the world.

   _____

5. I took my 10 trip to Mexico last year.

   _____

6. The book about the Aztecs is the 5 book I had to read for my class.

   _____

B. Write three new sentences using ordinal numbers.

   _____

   _____

   _____

UNIT 16

Why Are the Williams Sisters Good at Tennis?

BEFORE YOU READ

Answer these questions.

1. Who are some famous tennis players?
2. Is tennis popular in your country?
3. Do you like tennis? Why or why not?

Why Are the Williams Sisters Good at Tennis?

1 Venus and Serena Williams are two of the best **female** tennis players in the world. One expert said, "They're faster, stronger, and more powerful than any other women who play the game." But without their father to guide them, they probably would not know how to play tennis.

2 When Richard and Oracene Williams got married, Richard told his wife that he wanted to have five daughters. In 1978, Richard saw a woman win $22,000 in a tennis match. He decided he wanted his daughters to be tennis players, too. The three daughters he already had weren't interested in tennis, but Venus was born in 1980, and then Serena in 1981. Now he had five daughters and two more chances to have tennis players.

3 Richard Williams was not a wealthy man. He **dropped out of** high school at age sixteen. Then he and his wife started their family in Compton, California. This was not a nice place to live with a young family. "It was a dangerous **neighborhood**," said Richard. The only tennis courts were in a very bad area. Richard first taught himself to play, then he taught his two youngest daughters when they were about four years old.

4 Both girls liked tennis and were good at it. By age ten, Venus appeared on the front page of the *New York Times*. She was **number one** in Southern California for girls under twelve years old. Serena was number one for girls under ten. Richard decided it was time to find a real trainer for Venus and Serena. He moved the family to Florida and **enrolled** the girls in a tennis school. They played tennis six hours a day, six days a week, and also took regular classes.

5 At age fourteen, Venus started to play in **professional** tournaments and won her first professional match. Now Venus was playing tennis with world-famous players. She got a lot of **attention**. The **media** was interested in her for many reasons: her age, her sister, her father, and her personal style. She was easy to recognize because of her unique hairstyle. She wore beads in her hair—1,800 beads, which took ten hours to put in. The next year, 1994, the Reebok shoe company paid Venus $12 million for a five-year contract to represent their products. That same year, Serena started to play

(continued)

professionally, too. She also wore beads in her hair. Later, Venus lost **points** in a tennis match because the beads from her hair fell all over the tennis court. After that, both sisters took out their beads.

6 Venus and Serena Williams are on the **list** of the top female tennis players in the world. Because of this, they sometimes have to play against each other professionally. Sometimes Venus wins; sometimes Serena wins. Sometimes they play together in doubles matches. A doubles match has two players on each side of the court. Each set of players works as a team against the other. Venus and Serena became the first sisters team to win a professional doubles match. The sisters went on to represent the United States in Sydney, Australia, for the Summer Olympics of 2000. They won a gold medal for doubles, then Venus won another gold medal **on her own**.

7 The sisters are similar to each other in their personalities and their **athletic** ability. Both of them are intelligent and get good grades in school. Their parents always made them **spend** as much **time** on schoolwork as on tennis. Venus still studies French and German and wants to learn Italian. She also writes poetry and works in the fashion industry. Serena speaks Russian and French. She gave a **speech** in French when she was in Paris. Both girls like to show what they know. They publish a newsletter called the *Tennis Monthly Recap*. Now they are thinking about college.

8 Venus and Serena Williams are great athletes who win tournaments and gold medals. They have made a lot of money and are very famous— you can even buy Venus and Serena dolls. But which sister is the better tennis player? We will see.

VOCABULARY

MEANING

Write the correct words in the blanks.

list	neighborhood	speech	enrolled	points
professional	attention	female	athletic	media

1. Venus and Serena are two of the best women, or _____, tennis players in the world.

2. The area where they lived was dangerous. It was not a nice _____.

3. The girls joined the school as students. They _____ at the school in Florida.

4. Venus played tennis and got paid. It was her job. She played in _____ tournaments.

5. Venus was popular on television, in newspapers, and with the _____ in general.

6. When Venus started to play professionally, people noticed her. She got a lot of _____.

7. In tennis, the player with four _____ wins.

8. The two sisters have their names on the _____ of the top female players in the world.

9. The sisters have great ability in sports. They have _____ ability.

10. Serena spoke in French to a group of people. She made a _____.

WORDS THAT GO TOGETHER

Write the correct words in the blanks.

number one	dropped out of	on her own	spend time

1. Their father did not finish high school. He _____ high school at age sixteen.

2. Venus was the best tennis player for girls under twelve years old. She was _____.

3. The girls play tennis a lot, but they also _____ on their schoolwork.

4. The sisters often do things together. Sometimes one sister does something _____.

USE

Work with a partner to answer the questions. Use complete sentences.

1. Who is getting a lot of *attention* in the news today?
2. When did you *enroll* in this school?
3. Who is *number one* in your class?
4. What do you like to do *on your own*?
5. How do you feel when you give a *speech*?

COMPREHENSION

UNDERSTANDING THE READING

Circle the letter of the correct answer.

1. Venus and Serena's father _____.
   a. taught them to play tennis
   b. did not want them to play tennis
   c. never learned how to play tennis
   d. thought tennis was more important than school

2. Venus started to play in professional tournaments _____.
   a. after Serena
   b. before Serena
   c. at the same time as Serena
   d. at age sixteen

3. The Williams sisters _____.
   a. always play each other professionally
   b. are among the top female tennis players in the world
   c. never play together in doubles matches
   d. never win when they play alone

REMEMBERING DETAILS

Reread the passage and fill in the blanks.

1. Richard Williams told his wife he wanted to have _____.
2. Richard Williams taught his daughters to play tennis when they were _____ years old.
3. They moved from California to _____.
4. Venus wore _____ in her hair.
5. The two sisters were in the Summer Olympics of 2000 in _____, _____.
6. Venus studies _____ and _____.
7. Serena speaks _____ and _____.

MAKING INFERENCES

All of the statements below are true. Some of them are stated directly in the reading. Others can be inferred, or guessed, from the reading. Write _S_ for each stated fact. Write _I_ for each inference.

____ 1. Richard Williams wanted a better life for his daughters than he had.

____ 2. The girls' parents made them play a lot of tennis and study.

____ 3. The sisters want people to notice them.

____ 4. They could not wear beads in their hair because it was a problem on the court.

____ 5. Both sisters want to have careers after they stop playing tennis.

TELL THE STORY

Work with a partner or together as a class. Tell the story of the Williams sisters. Use your own words. Your partner or other students can ask questions about the story.

DISCUSSION

Discuss the answers to these questions with your classmates.

1. Do men and women play the same sports? What is a sport played only by women? What is a sport played only by men?
2. Do you think a woman can win against a man in a tennis game? Discuss.
3. What do you think about two sisters playing tennis against each other? What about brothers or sisters who want the same job, or boyfriend or girlfriend? Have you experienced this, or do you know someone who has?

WRITING

Write six sentences or a short paragraph about a special ability you have.

Example: *My special ability is not playing a sport. My special ability is playing the violin. I started to play at age five.*

_____

_____

_____

_____

_____

_____

SPELLING AND PUNCTUATION

SUFFIXES: *–LY*

We use the suffix *–ly* to change some adjectives into adverbs.

*That same year, Serena started to play professiona**ly**, too.*

We often make spelling changes when we use *–ly*.

When we add *–ly* to a word ending in *–le*, we drop the *–le* and add *–ly*.
*incredible + –ly = incredi**bly***

When we add *–ly* to a word ending in *–y*, we change the *–y* to *–i*, and add *–ly*.
*happy + –ly = happ**ily***

When we add *–ly* to a word ending in *–c*, we add *–al* before adding *–ly*.
*basic + –ly = basic**ally***

A. Circle the correctly spelled word in each group.

1. comfortablly   comfortably   comfortabily

2. comically   comicly   comicely

3. annualy   annually   annualily

4. sincerly   sincerally   sincerely

B. Change the underlined words to adverbs by adding _-ly_. Write the new adverbs on the lines. Remember that some words will have spelling changes.

1. The two sisters play more <u>powerful</u> than other women.

   _____

2. The two sisters are <u>equal</u> good.

   _____

3. Venus won the match <u>easy</u>.

   _____

4. The sisters <u>final</u> went to the Olympics.

   _____

5. The sisters practice <u>regular</u>.

   _____

6. They <u>usual</u> practice every day.

   _____

7. Without their father's help, they <u>probable</u> would not know how to play tennis.

   _____

8. Venus was first to win championships, but Serena <u>gradual</u> caught up with her.

   _____

C. Write three new sentences with adverbs ending in _-ly_.

_____

_____

_____

UNIT 17

Where Is Timbuktu?

BEFORE YOU READ

Answer these questions.

1. Where do you think Timbuktu is?
2. Do you think Timbuktu is a real place?
3. What kind of place do you think it is?

Where Is Timbuktu?

1 Many people believe Timbuktu is a place of **mystery**. It is a romantic land from **legends**. People often use Timbuktu as a symbol of a place that is far away, unknown, or difficult to reach. For example:

"I want to work in this office, but my company may send me to Timbuktu."

"Sorry I'm late. I had to park my car in Timbuktu!"

"I'm happy that you like your gift. I had to go to Timbuktu to find it."

2 Timbuktu is not only a symbol. It is also a real place. It is a city in the country of Mali in western Africa. Timbuktu is on the **edge** of the Sahara Desert, about eight miles from the Niger River. Even today it is not easy to travel there; the best way to get there is by river or camel. At one time, Timbuktu was a very important city, like Rome, Athens, or Jerusalem. It was the center of learning in Africa, and people called it the "City of Gold."

3 A group of **nomads** created Timbuktu in the twelfth century. By the fourteenth century, it was a center for the gold and salt **trade**. Everyone needed salt, so they charged a high price for it. Sometimes, salt was more expensive than gold! People outside the **region** started to hear and talk about Timbuktu when Mansa Moussa was Mali's king. His religion was Islam, and he built beautiful mosques and huge libraries to spread the religion. Timbuktu was also famous for its universities. The University of Sankore had 25,000 students. People called it the Oxford University of the Sahara. Moussa made Timbuktu into a cultural center for Islam. It became an important city **not just** in Africa, **but also** in the world of Islam.

4 Stories about the wealth of Timbuktu spread **far and wide**, and other kingdoms wanted it for themselves. In 1591, Morocco conquered Timbuktu and controlled it until 1780. During this time, they killed many of the students and teachers, closed the universities, **destroyed** trade, and did not take care of the city. Timbuktu was no longer the City of Gold. After the Moroccans, other African groups controlled Timbuktu.

5 In the late eighteenth and early nineteenth centuries, European countries began to make colonies in some parts of Africa. Europeans believed Timbuktu was a city covered in gold. They thought gold in

(continued)

Timbuktu was as **common** as sand! Europeans tried to reach Timbuktu again and again, but they weren't successful. They didn't know how to cross the Sahara Desert and survive where it was hot and there was no water. The men died of **thirst** and disease, or thieves killed them.

6 In 1824, The Geographical Society of Paris offered a prize of 100,000 francs to the first person who could **bring back** information about Timbuktu. Many people tried, but René Caillié was the first to reach Timbuktu and come back alive. He started on the coast of western Africa and traveled for a year. On the way, he learned to speak Arabic and dressed as an Arab. He finally arrived in Timbuktu in April 1828, but he couldn't believe his eyes. He saw a city of small houses made of earth— no buildings covered with gold. The economy of Timbuktu was dead, but the intellectual and religious life of the city continued to live. When the French colonized the area in 1894, more than twenty schools were still open and were doing very well.

7 Mali became an independent country in 1960. It is a poor country, and Timbuktu is a poor city. Some of the beautiful old buildings are still standing. Sankore University is still open, but today it has only about 15,000 students. In 1974, the government of Mali and UNESCO built a center to hold and preserve over 20,000 old documents from Timbuktu's libraries. These documents were copied by hand over many centuries and contain more than a thousand years of knowledge. It is extremely important to preserve these documents, because Timbuktu is **in danger**. The sand and winds from the Sahara are destroying the plants, the water, and the historic buildings. There is now a program to save the city and its history. People don't want Timbuktu to become only a legend again. Although it is hot, poor, and far away from everything, thousands of visitors come to this city of mystery every year.

VOCABULARY

MEANING

Write the correct words in the blanks.

common	destroyed	edge	region	trade
nomads	legends	mystery	thirst	

1. People don't know much about Timbuktu. It is a place of

   _____.

2. Timbuktu is a place of unreal stories of the past. It is a place of

   _____.

3. The city is on the border, or _____, of the desert.

4. People who travel from place to place without a permanent home are

   _____; at one time these people created Timbuktu.

5. People bought and sold gold and salt in Timbuktu. It was a center for the

   gold and salt _____.

6. The Moroccans damaged and harmed the salt and gold trade in

   Timbuktu. They _____ trade.

7. Everybody was interested in Timbuktu, including people who lived

   nearby and people who lived far away from the _____.

8. There was no water in the desert. The men died of _____.

9. There was gold everywhere in Timbuktu. Gold was _____.

WORDS THAT GO TOGETHER

Write the correct words in the blanks.

in danger	far and wide	bring back	not just . . . but also

1. The French gave a prize of 100,000 francs to the person who could go
   to Timbuktu, return to France, and _____ information.

2. Stories about the gold in Timbuktu went everywhere. The stories went

   _____.

3. Timbuktu is _____ hot, _____ poor.

4. Timbuktu may lose all of its old buildings. It is a bad situation. The city

   is _____.

USE

Work with a partner to answer the questions. Use complete sentences.

1. What is something *common* we use every day in school?

2. What is the best drink for *thirst*?

3. What do people *bring back* from vacation?

4. What television show or movie is a *mystery*?

5. What is the name of a famous *legend* or a person from a legend you know?

6. What *trade* is popular in your country?

COMPREHENSION

UNDERSTANDING THE READING

Circle the letter of the correct answer.

1. Timbuktu _____.

    a. is not a real place today

    b. is only a symbol of a faraway place

    c. is a country in Africa

    d. was an important city in the past

2. At one time, Timbuktu _____.

    a. was the cultural center for Islam

    b. controlled Morocco

    c. was made of gold

    d. was easy to travel to

3. Today, Timbuktu is _____.

    a. being destroyed by sand and wind

    b. a colony of the French

    c. a poor city that nobody visits

    d. being destroyed by visitors

REMEMBERING DETAILS

Reread the passage and fill in the blanks.

1. Timbuktu is on the edge of _____.
2. People called Timbuktu _____.
3. Mansa Moussa's religion was _____.
4. René Caillié dressed as _____.
5. Mali became an independent country in _____.
6. There is a center to preserve _____.

MAKING INFERENCES

All of the statements below are true. Some of them are stated directly in the reading. Others can be inferred, or guessed, from the reading. Write S for each stated fact. Write I for each inference.

_____ 1. Europeans wanted to colonize Timbuktu, but it was hard to get there.

_____ 2. The Moroccans didn't care about Timbuktu's culture.

_____ 3. At one time, Timbuktu was a rich city.

_____ 4. The University of Sankore was famous.

_____ 5. History is very important to the people of Timbuktu.

TELL THE STORY

Work with a partner or together as a class. Tell your partner the story of Timbuktu. Use your own words. Your partner or other students can ask questions about the story.

DISCUSSION

Discuss the answers to these questions with your classmates.

1. Would you like to visit Timbuktu? Why or why not?
2. What place or city do you dream of visiting one day?
3. What places, such as cities, monuments, or parks, are in danger today? What is being done to help them? What more can be done?

WRITING

Write six sentences or a short paragraph about a place you always wanted to go to.

Example: *My dream is to go to Paris one day. I hear stories about Paris. People say it is very romantic.*

_____

_____

_____

_____

_____

_____

SPELLING AND PUNCTUATION

ABBREVIATIONS

An *abbreviation* is a short way to write a word, a phrase, or a name. We cannot use abbreviations in every kind of writing. Abbreviations are common in advertisements, scientific and technical writing, and other places, such as telephone books.

In 1974, the government of Mali and UNESCO built a center to preserve documents.

There are several types of abbreviations.

- one, two, or three letters for a word
  page = p.   road = rd.   apartment = apt.

- the first letter of each word, each letter said separately

  U.S. = United States

  U.K. = United Kingdom

  B.A. = Bachelor of Arts (degree)

  M.A. = Master of Arts (degree)

  U.N. = United Nations

  CD = Compact Disc

The recent trend is to write abbreviations without periods, but it is acceptable to write many abbreviations both ways. If you are not sure, check your dictionary.

We may also use the first letter of each word to make a new word. These abbreviations do not use periods.

UNESCO = United Nations Educational, Scientific, and Cultural Organization

TOEFL = Test of English as a Foreign Language

NATO = North Atlantic Treaty Organization

There are many exceptions to these rules. Always check a dictionary or style book if you are not sure of an abbreviation.

Write the abbreviation next to each word. You may use a dictionary.

1. Avenue   _____

2. Mister   _____

3. World War II   _____

4. Boulevard   _____

5. Street   _____

6. miles per hour   _____

7. Medical Doctor   _____

8. Company   _____

9. Doctor   _____

10. Fahrenheit   _____

11. centimeter   _____

12. Automated Teller Machine   _____

UNIT 18

Where Do the Most Vegetarians Live?

BEFORE YOU READ

Answer these questions.

1. Do you know any vegetarians?
2. What do vegetarians eat?
3. Why are people vegetarians?

Where Do the Most Vegetarians Live?

1 Some people choose to be vegetarian, but others are vegetarian because of their religion, their culture, or the place they live. There are vegetarians all over the world, but the country with the most vegetarians is India.

2 About one billion people live in India, and most follow the Hindu religion. Hindus think it is wrong to kill or make animals **suffer**. They think if they do, they will suffer the same way **one day**. Hindus believe the cow is **sacred**; therefore, most Hindus do not eat beef. **In fact**, the Hindu word for cow, *aghnaya*, means "not to be killed."

3 There are different kinds of vegetarians in the world. Some vegetarians do not eat beef or red meat, but they eat chicken and fish. Some do not eat red meat, chicken, or fish but they eat cheese, butter, eggs, milk, and other animal **products**. Other vegetarians do not use anything that **comes from** an animal. Some don't wear wool because it harms the sheep, don't use silk because it hurts silkworms, and don't eat honey because they do not want to hurt bees. Other vegetarians only eat vegetables; however they do not kill plants. For example, they will not eat carrots or potatoes because when you pick them, the plant dies. They will eat apples or pears because picking them does not harm the plant. Some vegetarians do not kill or hurt any animal—not even a fly or a mosquito!

4 In India, too, there are different kinds of vegetarians. Some Hindus are **strict** vegetarians. Other Hindus eat all meat **except for** beef, but they only eat it about once a week. Many families eat chicken or lamb a few times a year at special occasions, like weddings. The Hindus of the upper **classes** do not eat meat or drink alcohol. However, the lower classes eat all meats except for beef. The upper classes, or *Brahmans*, cannot kill anything that is moving. If they do, they believe they will become that animal in their next lives and will be killed, too.

5 Hindus follow other rules when they eat. They **rinse** their mouths, arms, and legs before and after eating to clean themselves. It is a custom for the man of the house to eat thirty-two mouthfuls at each meal, chewing carefully and thinking about pleasant things. Strict Hindus do not eat garlic or onions. They believe that foods have characteristics. Some foods are "hot," others are "cold." They think the strong smells of

(continued)

these foods are too powerful for the **mild** tastes and smells of other vegetables. Also, in middle-class families, many women do not eat meat, but men do. Women think eating meat is something **masculine**. They also connect meat with **violence**.

6   Hindus also think it is lucky to eat with a person who is one hundred years old or a student, but should avoid eating with a bald person, an actor, an athlete, a musician, or a woman with a second husband. Strict Hindus also believe it is not correct for a wife to eat with her husband, but it is good if she eats the rest of his food after he finishes his meal. It is wrong for a Hindu to eat food that has stood overnight, has been cooked twice, or is left over from an earlier meal. Any food that has been touched by a foot, a person's clothing, or a dog cannot be eaten.

7   Vegetarians are everywhere in both rich and poor countries. In parts of the world such as Africa, the Middle East, and Southeast Asia, meat is uncommon, and therefore it is an easy choice to be vegetarian. Surveys show that in both the United States and Britain about 4 percent of the population is vegetarian. And more and more people are choosing vegetarianism every day. Many people become vegetarian for health reasons. They look and feel better when they stop eating meat. Some famous vegetarians include Leonardo da Vinci, Albert Einstein, Thomas Edison, Leo Tolstoy, Brad Pitt, Sylvester Stallone, Paul McCartney, Penelope Cruz, and Madonna.

VOCABULARY

MEANING

Write the correct words in the blanks.

suffer	sacred	violence	strict	mild
rinse	classes	masculine	products	

1.   Hindus do not kill cows because they believe cows are very, very special. They believe cows are _____.

2.   Hindus believe it is wrong to give pain to an animal and make it _____.

3. Some vegetarians don't eat anything that comes from an animal. They don't even eat animal _____, such as milk, cheese, and butter.

4. It is important for some Hindus to be clean before they eat so they _____ their mouths, arms, and legs with water.

5. Hindu people have different social levels, or _____, from lower to high or upper.

6. Some vegetarians follow all the rules very seriously. They are _____.

7. Some foods have a strong taste, other foods do not have a strong taste. They have a _____ taste.

8. Men have special qualities that only men have. These are _____ qualities.

9. When people hurt or kill, they use _____.

WORDS THAT GO TOGETHER

Write the correct words in the blanks.

in fact	except for	one day	comes from

1. A product such as milk _____ the cow.

2. Hindus believe that _____ they will come back to the world as a man or animal.

3. Not all Hindus are strict vegetarians. _____, some eat chicken or lamb a few times a year.

4. Some Hindus eat chicken and lamb. They eat all meat _____ beef.

USE

Work with a partner to answer the questions. Use complete sentences.

1. What are some milk *products* people eat?
2. What is something you usually *rinse*?
3. Is your teacher *strict*, not *strict*, or very *strict*?
4. What vegetable has a *mild* taste?
5. What movie star looks *masculine*?
6. What do you want to be *one day*?

COMPREHENSION

Circle the letter of the correct answer.

1. Vegetarians are _____.
    a. only in poor countries
    b. all over the world
    c. only in religious countries
    d. only in India, the United States, and Britain

2. Strict Hindu husbands and wives _____.
    a. never eat together
    b. always eat the same things
    c. connect meat with violence
    d. eat thirty-two mouthfuls at each meal

3. All over the world, _____.
    a. people are becoming vegetarian
    b. vegetarians are religious
    c. vegetarians follow the same rules
    d. there are more women vegetarians than men vegetarians

REMEMBERING DETAILS

Circle *T* if the sentence is true. Circle *F* if the sentence is false.

1.	Some vegetarians do not wear wool.	T	F
2.	Strict vegetarians do not eat potatoes.	T	F
3.	Two percent of Americans are vegetarian.	T	F
4.	It is lucky for a Hindu to eat with a bald person.	T	F
5.	Strict Hindus do not eat onions.	T	F
6.	Rich countries do not have vegetarians.	T	F

MAKING INFERENCES

All of the statements below are true. Some of them are stated directly in the reading. Others can be inferred, or guessed, from the reading. Write *S* for each stated fact. Write *I* for each inference.

_____ 1. Many intelligent people choose to be vegetarian.

_____ 2. Hindus are vegetarian because of their religion.

_____ 3. Many Americans become vegetarian for health reasons.

_____ 4. Vegetarianism is growing because meat may cause some illnesses.

_____ 5. In some parts of the world, people are vegetarian because there is no meat for them to eat.

TELL THE STORY

Work with a partner or together as a class. Tell the story of vegetarians. Use your own words. Your partner or other students can ask questions about the story.

DISCUSSION

Discuss the answers to these questions with your classmates.

1. Do you think it is good for your health to be a vegetarian? Why or why not?
2. What are some rules about food in some religions?
3. Do you think it is right for strict vegetarian parents to raise their children as vegetarians too?

WRITING

Write six sentences or a short paragraph about the kinds of foods you eat.

Example: *I am not a vegetarian. I eat meat, fish, and animal products because I think they are good for you.*

_____

_____

_____

_____

_____

_____

SPELLING AND PUNCTUATION

SUFFIXES: *–IST*, *–ER*, *–OR*, *–AN*, AND *–IAN*

We add the suffixes *–ist*, *–er*, *–or*, *–an*, or *–ian* to nouns or verbs to describe the person associated with certain things and places.

vegetable	vegeta**rian**	a person who eats vegetables
India	Ind**ian**	a person who lives in India
farm	farm**er**	a person who works on a farm

A. **All the people below are vegetarians. Write their jobs on the lines. You may use a dictionary.**

1. Thomas Edison was an _____ (a person who invents).

2. Marc Anthony is a _____ (a person who sings).

3. Leonardo da Vinci was a _____ (a person who paints).

4. Paul McCartney is _____ (a person who plays music).

5. He is also a _____ (a person who composes music).

6. Brad Pitt is an _____ (a person who acts).

7. Leo Tolstoy was a _____ (a person who writes books).

8. Albert Einstein was _____ (person who does work in science).

9. Pythagoras was a _____ (a person who studies mathematics).

10. Yehudi Menuhin is a _____ (a person who plays the violin).

B. **Write three new sentences using the suffixes above.**

_____

_____

_____

SELF-TEST 2
Units 10–18

A. SENTENCE COMPLETION

Circle the letter of the correct answer.

1. _____, the parents took it to the priest.
   a. As soon as baby was born
   b. As soon as a baby was born
   c. As soon as a baby is born
   d. As soon as baby born

2. _____ that is a little different.
   a. Koreans Americans have a ceremony
   b. Korean Americans have ceremony
   c. Korean Americans have a ceremony
   d. Korean American have a ceremony

3. One wrestler may finish the ceremony in one minute, while _____ two minutes.
   a. another may take
   b. another may takes
   c. the another may take
   d. other may take

4. Stephen King _____ American writer to this day.
   a. sold more books than any other
   b. has sold more books than any other
   c. has sold more book than any other
   d. sold more books than any others

5. Hundreds of years ago, _____ thing a person owned.
   a. a bed was the most valuable
   b. a bed was the valuablest
   c. a bed was most valuable
   d. bed was the more valuable

6. Cortés and his men _____ when they first arrived in what is today Mexico.
   a. were lucky
   b. was lucky
   c. were luck
   d. had lucky

7. The two sisters are great athletes _____ and gold medals.
   a. which win tournaments
   b. who win tournaments
   c. who tournaments win
   d. who tournament win

8. At one time, Timbuktu _____ that salt was more expensive than gold.
   a. have so much gold
   b. had so much gold
   c. had so many gold
   d. had so much golds

9. Strict _____.
   a. vegetarian only eat vegetables
   b. vegetarians only eat vegetable
   c. vegetarians only they eat vegetables
   d. vegetarians only eat vegetables

B. VOCABULARY

Complete the definitions. Circle the letter of the correct answer.

1. Even thousands of years ago, the calendar of the Aztecs was _____ and had 365 days.
   a. national   b. accurate   c. brave   d. neutral

2. In the past, Korean parents did not find a marriage partner for their children themselves. They found a matchmaker and _____ her to do the job.
   a. recognized   b. apologized   c. hired   d. represented

3. Sumo wrestlers can move in any position. They are _____.
   a. harmful   b. flexible   c. accurate   d. basic

4. When Stephen King was a boy, his mother wanted and _____ him to write stories and send them to publishers.
   a. complained   b. predicted   c. encouraged   d. recovered

5. Some people put something to drink near their bed _____ they got thirsty at night.
   a. was a sign of   b. according to   c. kind of   d. in case

6. It was a _____ that Cortés came in the year predicted for the Feathered Serpent to come back.
   a. contest   b. coincidence   c. possession   d. ceremony

7. The Williams sisters _____ at a school in Florida.
   a. enrolled   b. reached   c. preserved   d. retired

8. In Timbuktu, there was gold everywhere at one time. Gold was as _____ as sand.
   a. strict   b. common   c. strange   d. scary

9. One Hindu rule is to _____ your mouth, arms, and legs with water before and after you eat.
   a. press   b. mix   c. rinse   d. raise

C. SPELLING AND PUNCTUATION

Circle the letter of the sentence with the correct spelling and punctuation.

1. a. 2,600 years ago, the Mayans had a calendar with 365 days.

    b. Two thousand six hundred years ago, the Mayans had a calendar with three hundred and sixty five days.

    c. 2,600 years ago. the Mayans had a calendar with 365 days.

    d. Two thousand six hundred years ago, the Mayans had a calendar with 365 days.

2. a. A Korean wedding dessert has three main ingredients: raisins, chestnuts, and pine nuts.

    b. A Korean wedding dessert has three main ingredients raisins, chestnuts, and pine nuts.

    c. A Korean wedding dessert has three main ingredients, raisins, chestnuts, and pine nuts.

    d. A Korean wedding dessert has three main ingredients. Raisins, chestnuts, and pine nuts.

3. a. A young man must be 200 lbs. and 5 ft. 7 in. tall to join a sumo stable.

    b. A young man must be 200 pounds and 5 feet seven in. tall to join a sumo stable.

    c. A young man must be two hundred pounds and five feet seven inches tall to join a sumo stable.

    d. A young man must be two hundred lbs. and five feet seven in. tall to join a sumo stable.

4. a. Stephen King's books were made into movies like "The Shining" and "Carrie."

    b. Stephen King's books were made into movies like *The Shining* and *Carrie*.

    c. Stephen King's books were made into movies like _The Shining_ and _Carrie_.

    d. Stephen King's books were made into movies like The Shining and Carrie.

5. a. In, ancient Rome people went to bed in their day clothes.

   b. In ancient Rome people went to bed, in their day clothes.

   c. In ancient Rome, people went to bed in their day clothes.

   d. In ancient Rome people went to bed in their day clothes.

6. a. Cortés went to Mexico for the 1 time in 1519.

   b. Cortés went to Mexico for the 1st time in 1519.

   c. Cortés went to Mexico for the first time in 1519.

   d. Cortés went to Mexico for the first time in fifteen nineteen.

7. a. The Williams sisters play equalely well.

   b. The Williams sisters play equaly well.

   c. The Williams sisters, play equallly well.

   d. The Williams sisters play equally well.

8. a. People from the u.s. and the u.k. visit Timbuktu.

   b. People from the US and Uk visit Timbuktu.

   c. People from the U.S. and the U.K. visit Timbuktu.

   d. People from the us and the uk visit Timbuktu.

9. a. Paul McCartney is a musicist, a singer, a composer, and a vegetarian.

   b. Paul McCartney is a musician, a singer, a composist, and a vegetarian.

   c. Paul McCartney is a musician, a singor, a composer, and a vegetarian.

   d. Paul McCartney is a musician, a singer, a composer, and a vegetarian.

APPENDICES

WORD LIST

UNIT 1

Vocabulary

		Words that Go Together
arranged	partners	by hand
backward	pressed	had no idea
borrowed	rare	over and over
broke	statue	took . . . to court
effect		

UNIT 2

Vocabulary

		Words that Go Together
admire	limit	doesn't mind
afford	mat	doing their duty
contest	responsible	in the old days
enormous	slim	kinds of
future		

UNIT 3

Vocabulary

		Words that Go Together
brave	represent	give up
collection	souvenirs	look like
costumes	sword	set of
doll	third	take a bath
national		

UNIT 4

Vocabulary

		Words that Go Together
adventures	prisoner	passed the time
coast	reached	passed through
describes	romantic	settle down
guide	title	went to war
invited		

UNIT 5

Vocabulary

		Words that Go Together
already	race	no sign of
extreme	survived	on its way
fuel	voyage	used to
goal	whether	worked his way up
instead		

UNIT 6

Vocabulary

		Words that Go Together
hospitals	receive	came up with
injured	satisfied	first-aid kit
minister	service	got in touch with
pills	truck	had an accident

UNIT 7

Vocabulary

		Words that Go Together
preserve	tight	at last
recognize	treasures	believed in
spirit	tunnels	in the shape of
steal	wax	such as
thieves		

UNIT 8

Vocabulary

		Words that Go Together
harmful	sour	fell in love
noticed	trouble	got well
sciences	weak	made a name for himself
solution	worried	was interested in

UNIT 9

Vocabulary

		Words that Go Together
apologized	knocked	gave birth to
complain	neighbor	have respect for
effective	poor	in the thirteenth century
escape	youth	no word from

UNIT 10

Vocabulary

		Words that Go Together
accurate	including	a sign of
civilization	neutral	according to
descendants	permanently	bring up
destiny	predicted	got married
height		

UNIT 11

Vocabulary

		Words that Go Together
banquet	exchange	get engaged
ceremony	hired	in-law
deliver	match	set a date
document	shout	take a sip

UNIT 12

Vocabulary

		Words that Go Together
average	raise	chase away
basic	ranks	clap their hands
fist	retire	gain weight
flexible	serve	stamp their feet
origin		

UNIT 13

Vocabulary

		Words that Go Together
abandoned	persuaded	as usual
earn	recovered	line up
encouraged	scary	from place to place
fancy	trash	threw away
		went straight

UNIT 14

Vocabulary

		Words that Go Together
adjustable	necessary	in case
choices	possession	it was only after
especially	privacy	keep warm
fold	wealth	

UNIT 15

Vocabulary

		Words that Go Together
capital	meanwhile	calm down
coincidence	mix	dedicated to
colony	sacrificed	have a chance
conquer	strange	in their favor
independent	terrible	watched over

UNIT 16

Vocabulary

		Words that Go Together
athletic	media	dropped out of
attention	neighborhood	number one
enrolled	points	on her own
female	professional	spend time
list	speech	

UNIT 17

Vocabulary

		Words that Go Together
common	nomads	bring back
destroyed	region	far and wide
edge	thirst	in danger
legends	trade	not just . . . but also
mystery		

UNIT 18

Vocabulary

		Words that Go Together
classes	sacred	comes from
masculine	strict	except for
mild	suffer	in fact
products	violence	one day
rinse		

MAP OF THE WORLD

N = north
E = east
S = south
W = west

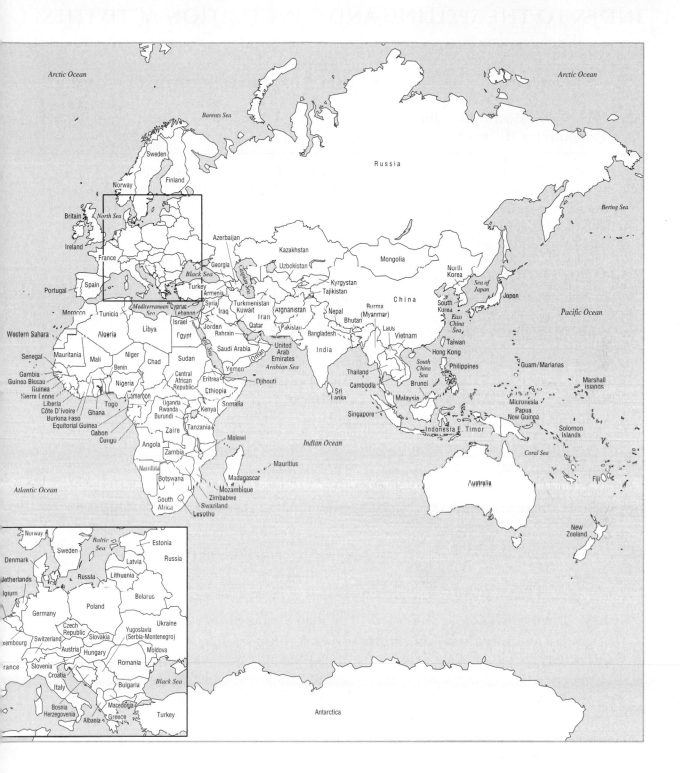

INDEX TO THE SPELLING AND PUNCTUATION ACTIVITIES